VINTAGE
BEER

VINTAGE BEER

A Taster's Guide to Brews That Improve over Time

PATRICK DAWSON

Storey Publishing

The mission of Storey Publishing is to serve our customers by
publishing practical information that encourages
personal independence in harmony with the environment.

Edited by Margaret Sutherland
Art direction by Cynthia N. McFarland
Cover design by Alethea Morrison
Book design by Tom Morgan of Blue Design

Photography by © Lightbox Images Photography, Images by Thomas Cooper, except
for Mars Vilaubi, front cover; © Patrick Dawson, vi, 23, 32, 38, 78; © Kathy Wright/
Alamy, 18; © Adam Henderson, 52; © Studioschulz.com, 53; © Charles D. Cook/
DrinkBelgianBeer.com, 133; courtesy of the Beer Judge Certification Program, 139

Indexed by Nancy D. Wood

Storey Publishing
210 MASS MoCA Way
North Adams, MA 01247
www.storey.com

Storey Publishing is committed to
making environmentally responsible
manufacturing decisions. This book
was printed on paper made from
sustainably harvested fiber.

Printed in China by Shenzhen Caimei Printing Co., Ltd.
10 9 8 7 6 5 4 3 2 1

LIBRARY OF CONGRESS CATALOGING-IN-PUBLICATION DATA
Dawson, Patrick, 1982-
  Vintage beer / by Patrick Dawson.
     pages cm
  Includes index.
  ISBN 978-1-61212-156-7 (pbk. : alk. paper)
  ISBN 978-1-61212-384-4 (ebook)
  1. Beer. I. Title.
TP577.D35 2014
663'.42--dc23

2013040101

CONTENTS

Foreword viii

Introduction: The World of Vintage Beer 1

Chapter 1: The Aging Beer 9
Vintage Beer Rules

Chapter 2: Determining Vintage Potential 17
*Malt · Hops · Yeast Esters and Phenols · Alcohol · Wood ·
Oxidation · Microbiota*

Chapter 3: The Best Beer Styles for Your Cellar 59
*English Barley Wines · American Barley Wines · Imperial Stouts ·
Belgian Quads · Flanders Red and Brown Ales · Gueuzes*

Chapter 4: Tasting Classic Cellar Beers 83

Chapter 5: Dark and Cool: Selecting Your Cellar 111
Temperature · Light Exposure · Humidity · Cellar Configurations

Chapter 6: How to Manage Your Cellar 121
Paper Journal · Spreadsheet · Cellar Apps

Appendix: Outstanding Vintage-Beer Bars 128
*Toronado · Bull & Bush Brewery · Falling Rock Taphouse ·
Ebenezer's Restaurant & Pub · Cafe Kulminator · Brick Store Pub ·
Brouwer's Cafe · Akkurat Restaurant & Bar · Monk's Cafe · Delilah's*

References 138

Glossary 140

Index 143

"You cellar and drink 10-year-old beers? Are you crazy?"

I can't tell you how many times over the last three decades I have had people ask me this very question. Well, the answer is: I'm not crazy, and neither are the legions of beer fans who have started aging beers. Of course, I'm not talking about those fizzy, yellow, lowest-common-denominator beers. You know — the ones where the cans change color when the beer is cold enough. Sometimes they're sold in 30-packs. I'm talking about craft beer, made with the best ingredients; if adjuncts are added, they are there to enhance the flavor, not lighten it. Even among these craft beers, less than five percent of everything produced is appropriate for aging. Most are meant to be consumed as fresh as possible, whether they are hoppy IPAs, cloudy hefeweizens, or crisp, well-crafted pilsners. The styles you will find in this book are beers that can age like a fine wine — old ales, imperial stouts, gueuzes, Belgian quads, and many more.

I've been aging beers since the late seventies; my cellar has included 2,500 beers for the last 25 years. I've either written or been interviewed for a number of articles on the subject. It became my obsession to travel the world, meet like-minded individuals, and discuss the principles of aging beer over glasses of vintage ales and lagers too numerous to count. During those trips I've sampled nineteenth-century English ales and 50-year-old lambics.

I've held vertical tastings of Thomas Hardy's Ale from 1968 through 2001. Sometimes the vintage beers are amazing, and sometimes they're well past their prime. One thing they have all held in common for me was the excitement of opening the bottle and smelling and tasting a bit of history.

Over the last five years there have been a growing number of websites and forums out there on the Internet that feature supposed experts claiming to know everything there is to know about aging beers. Some are better than others, but all are lacking a complete knowledge of the subject. Not until I met Patrick Dawson, a few years ago, had I found someone with enough determination, passion, and will to research the subject so completely as to be able to write the seminal book on aging beers. *Vintage Beer* will take you on a journey that includes identifying the correct beers to age, understanding the aging process, creating your own cellar, and finally, enjoying the fruits of your labor. Discover the aroma and flavor nuances that can be found in a well-aged beer.

"Dr." Bill Sysak
Craft Beer Ambassador
Stone Brewing Co.

The World of Vintage Beer

First things first, grab a beer and settle in. I firmly believe that when you're reading and learning about beer, you should be drinking and experiencing beer. It's a truly beautiful cerebral-sensory experience. Okay, continue.

It had been a long night of drinking. I wasn't long out of college, but the late-night beer binges were already beginning to wear on me. I was at a point in my life where I was starting to opt for quality over quantity, and while taking a swig in the wee hours I would find myself thinking about how I was going to feel the next day rather than what I should drink next. My homebrew club's meeting was reaching one of those epic nights that always seemed to happen in December when everyone was more excited about drinking "just one more" beer rather than facing the snowy, cold walk home. I'd had enough, though, and was just announcing that I was heading out when the host insisted I stay since she was going to open something special.

That month's meeting host, Maggie, worked at one of the best new wine stores in town, Mondo Vino, but her true passion was beer. Before discovering this shop, I had been choosing what I thought were exotic imports, like Dos Equis and Heineken, over Coors Light and fancied myself quite the beer snob. The first time I walked into the store, though, she quickly put me in my place in just about every aspect of beer (not that that was very hard to do at the time). I credit her with helping to push me onto the path of seeking and appreciating truly good beer. Anyway, years later, experience told me that when Maggie was excited about a beer, it was well worthwhile to sit back and wait for your glass to be filled. So when she announced that,

> **What greeted my nose when I lifted that glass was something that I will always remember.**

as a Christmas gift, her boss had given her a magnum of Duvel that, she added triumphantly, "had been aged for three years!" I was more than a little flabbergasted.

Now, I had vague notions of aged beers, but they were, in my mind, dusty little bottles of British beers that, I figured, people kept more for their collectability than for there being anything particularly special in them. I just couldn't comprehend why anyone would take a world-class brew like Duvel and ruin it by letting it get skunky and flat. And an entire magnum at that! Fighting the urge to roll my eyes, I proffered my glass and decided the high ABV (alcohol by volume) would at least keep me warm on the walk home.

What greeted my nose when I lifted that glass was something that I will always remember. Overwhelmed by the complex bouquet of fruit aromas, I struggled to pinpoint all that I was taking in. There was grape, pineapple, and maybe even a little kiwi in there. In a young Duvel, they're in the background and overshadowed by the hop profile, but in the aged beer they burst to the front in a vibrant sweetness. I wanted to shrink myself down and spend the rest of my life in that glass. How had this happened? Convinced that any flavor had disappeared into the potent aroma, I took a sip still expecting to taste a stale old beer.

What I encountered instead was a slight caramel sweetness that played off the beer's crisp acidity, and I was surprised that the alcohol heat had disappeared. I was astounded. All my experience up to that point, albeit limited, had taught me that beer was a beverage that was meant to be drunk fresh. That was why you got beer from the brewery. That was why you always

The prominent alcohol nose of certain beers fades after a few years, allowing the beer to develop complexities.

Two excellent beers that taste best at opposite ends of the aging spectrum: Hopslam should be drunk fresh, and Thomas Hardy's Ale should be aged as long as patience allows.

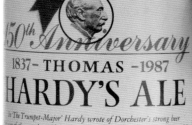

STRONGEST BEER
IN BRITAIN

The British beers bottled with its natural
able for at least 25 years if stored at 52°
ned before drinking, stand for 48 hour
atment to settle and then pour carefu

150th Anniversary

1837 - THOMAS - 1987

HARDY'S ALE

In 'The Trumpet-Major' Hardy wrote of Dorchester's strong beer
was of the most beautiful colour that the eye of an artist in beer could
desire; full in body, yet brisk as a volcano; piquant, yet without a
twang; luminous as an autumn sunset; free from streakiness of taste
but finally, rather heady.

BOTTLE Nº A 1204

Brewed and Bottled by Bière de Luxe brassée et mise en bouteilles par
ELDRIDGE, POPE & CO. plc · DORCHESTER · DORSET · ENGLAND

33 cl 'e'

HOPSLAM
ALE

NET CONTENTS
12 FL OZ 355 ML

BELL'S HOPSLAM

ALE

ALE BREWED WITH HONEY

...d and Bottled by Bell's Brewery, Inc., Comstock, MI 49053 checked the expiration date. My world was turned upside down. I had been doing it all wrong!

The years that followed were interesting, to say the least. I became obsessed with aging beer. I adopted the logic that all beer must get better over time. I figured that if wine improved with age, so would beer. (I found out later that not all wines improve with age.) I waited as patiently as I could for my bottles to turn into something like the heavenly nectar I had tasted that night.

With only a few exceptions, the results were disastrous. I would triumphantly pull five-year-old bottles of Fat Tire from the cellar expecting a masterpiece, only to end up with an overly sweet beer with weird off-tastes. The hops that I love

My early cellaring results were mostly disastrous.

so much in an IPA (India pale ale) were all but gone, leaving a thin malty mess. All my cherished beers came out tasting like wet cardboard — it was heartbreaking. Each one of those beers had become a little friend I was eagerly waiting to meet again, and they were all ruined. Nonetheless, I did end up with a few beers that were intriguing enough to make me want to continue the experiment — but only after I knew what I was doing.

Not that there is a wealth of information out there now (which is probably why you're reading this), but back then there was absolutely no information about aging beer. There was no beeradvocate.com Cellaring/Aging Beer forum. There was word-of-mouth and experimentation, and that was about it. So I asked. A lot. I put questions to anyone who would listen. I talked to brewers to try to find out what they did differently when planning a vintage brew. I found other hobbyists who aged beer and learned from their experiences. I traveled to Europe again and again and drank some of the great vintages those amazing geniuses had had the foresight to hoard decades ago.

What I eventually found out is that every beer is highly time dependent. Each beer has a "window" in which it can really shine. Finding that window takes a critical review of a beer's current qualities and the knowledge of how they (might) change. What you have to keep in mind, though, something it took me a while to figure out, is that everyone's optimal window is different, and it requires knowing what you are looking for in a beer. Some people may find that they love the spicy yeast notes that stand out in a Schneider Aventinus wheat doppelbock at around one year of age, while others will prefer how those flavors suggest vanilla at the four-year mark.

When critically reviewing the qualities of a beer over time, what most people find is that many beers' optimal time frame is as fresh as possible, while a small minority of beers benefit from a couple of months to a year of aging. There are only a select few that fall into the category of benefiting from multiple years of cellaring. I would put the number at something like 1 percent of all craft beers currently being brewed. When considering this optimal time frame, most will find that a two-week-old Bell's Hopslam double IPA is on a par with a 20-year-old vintage Thomas Hardy's Ale barley wine in the sense that they're both world-class brews being consumed at their peak ages.

So you might ask, why go to the trouble of aging beer? Well, the answer is very simple: aging beer allows time for various flavors not immediately present to develop and meld. With experience and knowledge, your nose and tongue learn to detect different aromatic and taste aspects in a beer and judge whether changes in them would make the beer more enjoyable. This book gives you the background knowledge you need to get started. As for the experience, well, that work is up to you alone, so start those arm curls.

Aging beer allows time for various flavors not immediately present to develop and meld.

What, then, do you need to know for your analyses? First, we'll discuss the aspects that are paramount in determining whether a beer might be a good candidate for cellaring. We'll talk about traditional aging mechanisms. Many you may already know, such as how hop bitterness fades linearly over time, but others might be new to you. How, for instance, a harsh, boozy flavor in a young beer is actually a good thing if it's to be aged. All these mechanisms are presented in simple-to-follow "vintage beer rules."

Next on the agenda is an in-depth look at the reasons behind these rules. Many of you will immediately flip to the next chapter, and probably be no worse off for it. But you science types in the group can take pride in the fact that you will know that the boozy nose on your three-year-old North Coast Old Stock was replaced by a nutty sweetness because the fusel alcohols present transferred electrons to the malt melanoidins, creating aldehydes. The rest of you can just make a mental note and be happy it happened.

Once you have built a solid knowledge base, it will be time to start applying it to real-world experience and actually tasting these beers that you have been anxiously awaiting. Tasting techniques along with anticipated flavors and aromas and their expected change over time are discussed to help guide you through this experience.

Finally, what to look for when determining the best place and way to cellar your beers is taken up. Whether you live in a 500-square-foot studio apartment or in an off-the-grid cabin in the middle of nowhere, optimal cellar conditions can be achieved. In addition, this book gives you information on ways to manage and track your growing collection.

To help with the learning process, I've included an entire chapter listing some examples of common, yet exceptional, brews that are considered benchmarks for what their beer style can achieve with time. You'll find graphs that show flavor changes over time based on vertical tastings by a panel of experienced beer tasters. With only a glance at the page, you'll learn what took us years of patient trial to determine.

Don't want to wait years to be able to drink these vintage brews? At the back of the book there is information on some of the finest vintage-beer bars in the world, where you can, for a small premium, take a shortcut to tasting some of the beers you've read so much about. Be sure to thank the geniuses who had the foresight to cellar these beers years before.

So on with it! This book is all about time, and time is a-wasting! A few years from now, on a cold winter night when you're savoring that smooth, cherry-soaked, chocolaty, bread pudding–esque vintage bottle of Trappistes Rochefort 10 from your cellar, you'll thank me. I promise.

CHAPTER 1

The Aging Beer

What is wonderful about the aging of beer is the fact that the results are relatively repeatable. Year to year, or more appropriately batch to batch, variations in a beer are fairly minor (with the exception of wild or lambic styles), which enables an experienced beer connoisseur to have a fairly good idea of what the brew will do as it ages. Wine, on the other hand, is nature's roulette wheel, spinning out a completely different beverage every year. A wine's change is somewhat unpredictable and may, or may not, improve over time, but it will definitely not improve in the same way each year. Yet there are in the world countless private and commercial cellars stocked with wine, and not beer.

There are a few reasons that collectors choose wine over beer for their cellars. Possibly the most important factor is that for a fermented beverage to age well, it needs to be made with top-quality ingredients and utmost care. Sadly, this is something that the brewing industry largely ignored in the not-so-distant past, opting to create bland, dull lagers instead of the rich barley wines and doppelbocks of yore. The wine industry, on the other hand, has continued to improve its product every year, making the most of technology and science in its pursuit of the highest possible quality. This difference is due mostly to the willingness of the average consumer to spend a considerably higher amount of money on wine than on beer. Beer has been viewed as a cheap, after-work quaff, not something to be savored and enjoyed with a meal. Luckily, times have changed, and people are now spending more on beer in return for a better product, which has persuaded brewers to produce better and better beers every year.

With this new wave of brews have come many that, though good or even great fresh, show the potential to get even better with age. But why is that, many will ask. There are several reasons. Some beers just need a little time to meld, much like letting a stew sit overnight to bring the flavors together. Others need time to allow some of their initial harsh flavors (booziness, for example) to take on a more complementary, enjoyable character. The main reason, however, is to give new flavors a chance to emerge. These flavors can sometimes take years to surface, but they're capable of elevating many already great beers to a level vying with the finest vintage wines, and at a fraction of the cost.

So, how do you know how a beer might age? What flavors might emerge? Which aspects will mellow and integrate? What else do you need to watch out for? Yes, there are a lot of questions out there. So many, in fact, that I think the best way to start answering them is to begin with some general guidelines to help you form a picture of a beer that will age well. Give the following fourteen "rules" a read, and you'll begin to understand what's most important when choosing and developing vintage beers. If you still find yourself asking why, the next chapter takes up in depth the apparent mysteries of aging beer.

VINTAGE BEER RULES

RULE No. 1: Unless the beer is smoked or sour, the alcohol content should be at least 8 percent ABV.
Alcohol acts as a preservative, slowing the effects of aging and buying time for those pleasant matured flavors to surface. Sour and smoked beers are exceptions because they have other preservatives (lactic acid and smoke phenols) to take the place of high alcohol content.

RULE No. 2: A beer's booziness eventually mellows and creates new, aging-derived flavors.

The fusel alcohols so harsh in many fresh high-ABV beers mellow over time and develop a wide variety of new flavors, ranging from sweet (toffee and caramel) to fruity (apricot and grape).

RULE No. 3: Darker malts create sherry and port flavors with age.

This point is key since sherry and port flavors are crucial aspects of the successful aging of many beers. Amber-colored beers develop sweet, sherrylike notes, while stouts, with their initial highly roasted flavors, turn chocolaty and portlike.

Because of its smoked malt, Alaskan Brewing Company's Smoked Porter ages well despite a 6.5 percent ABV.

RULE No. 4: Malt proteins drop out, causing a beer's body to slowly thin.

The loss of malt proteins and thinning of a beer's body is usually a disadvantage, so ageable beers should be very full-bodied up front. In the first few years of aging, some beers seem to thicken and become syrupy, but this actually indicates the emergence of new, sweet-tasting flavors (from aging alcohols) rather than an increase in a beer's viscosity.

RULE No. 5: Cloudy wheat proteins fall out quickly (after six months or so), leaving a clear, thinner beer.

Because of a tendency to lose a crucial component of their overall makeup, wheat beers, unless they have other aspects to help them age well, don't make good candidates for cellaring. Wheat beers are also often high in lipids, which create stale flavors as they age.

Very old beers can pour chunks of coagulated proteins that have formed in the bottom of the bottle.

RULE No. 6: Hoppiness fades over time and leaves behind either good or bad flavors, depending on the type of hops used.

Hops, which are so integral to many beers, slowly lose their effects with the passage of time. This applies to hop bitterness as well as to hop flavors and aromas. As they disappear, new flavors can appear in their place. American hops, which are high in alpha acids, often leave behind stale, papery flavors that can ruin a beer. Because of this, many beers, like IPAs, don't age well. On the other hand, European hops, high in beta acids, maintain their bitterness much longer over time and can even introduce enjoyable, fruity flavors suggestive of pineapple, cherry, or even wine.

RULE No. 7: Fruity yeast esters are volatile and change over time.

Given a few years, the tree-fruit esters (apple, pear, apricots) found in many Belgian and English-style beers will develop into dried-fruit flavors (raisin, fig, date). The banana-like esters typical of German wheat beers tend to fade and disappear quickly. Esters produced by certain strains of *Brettanomyces* (a genus of yeast, often abbreviated as "brett") are slow to develop but can create floral, pineapple, and grapefruit notes that are surprisingly resilient.

RULE No. 8: Spicy yeast phenols (pepper, clove, and smoke) develop into vanilla, leather, and tobacco flavors when aged.

The earthy flavors associated with the yeast phenols characteristic of many Belgian beers (and some German wheat beers) can develop into unique, complex flavors attainable only through patient cellaring. The smoky aspects of rauchbiers age similarly.

RULE No. 9: Oak-derived flavors from wood or barrel aging stay fairly constant over time.

A rare consistent aspect of vintage beer, oak flavors sometimes become overwhelming as the other flavors "tighten" with age. Although slowly, changes do occur as the vanilla flavors eventually disappear and the cinnamon notes increase. Coconut maintains a steady presence.

RULE No. 10: Sour beers (lambics, gueuzes, Flanders red ale) soften over time.

The sourness from the lactic acid that is so dominant in so-called sour beers when fresh (which often increases the first few years in the bottle) very slowly mellows in time. This can lead to a more elegant, complex beer as the other flavors are given a chance to assert themselves. Sometimes, very old sour beers taste more sour because all the other complementary flavors have diminished so much.

RULE No. 11: *Brettanomyces* yeasts continue to ferment in the bottle, creating more phenols over time and a drier beer.

Brett has experienced a massive surge in use in recent years. Such beers show a huge change when cellared. During aging, this slow-acting yeast will eat any and all available sugars, creating a very dry beer and often producing unique, though potentially overwhelming, phenolic flavors. Brett also consumes the residual oxygen in the bottle, so these beers are usually low in typical oxidation flavors.

RULE No. 12: Unpasteurized beers are preferred because the yeast in the bottle helps them develop and integrate better over time.

Beers bottled with their own unfiltered, unpasteurized yeast are a dynamic entity, able initially to consume residual oxygen and continue to slowly condition. Some nonliving beers can still age well, but they tend to have a more limited potential. It should be noted, though, that with enough time, the dead yeast cells at the bottom of a bottle-conditioned beer will deteriorate in a process called autolysis, which creates flavors as varied as blood, rust, or teriyaki. When and to what degree these flavors develop depends on a variety of factors, but the higher a beer's acidity (dark malts), ABV, storage temperature, or pressure, the more likely autolysis is to occur.

RULE No. 13: Beers should be cellared below their fermentation temperature (65°F/18°C for ales, 50°F/10°C for lagers).

Cellaring beer at the appropriate temperature allows it to remain in its natural state. Too hot, and new chemical processes start to occur, leading to unexpected, often bad flavors. Too cold, and the beer will develop at a crawl, which can halt some of the beer's natural processes. Staying 10°F (5°C) below fermentation temperature seems to optimize development, making a 55°F (13°C) cellar ideal for ales, which comprise the vast majority of vintage beers.

RULE No. 14: **A bottle's size and closure type affect the rate at which it ages.**

The larger the bottle, the more slowly the beer will age. In addition, different closure types can allow varying amounts of oxygen ingress, thereby affecting the aging rate. Caps are generally the most secure, with corks close behind, and swing tops a distant third.

Knowing these rules and applying them when choosing beers to age will enable you to build up a respectable cellar without too many regrettable choices. To have stronger confidence in your cellaring decisions, though, it's best to understand a bit more about the science that backs up these rules. Read on to gain a deeper understanding of the transformation that occurs within an aging beer.

Aged lambics display an array of subtle flavors.

CHAPTER 2

Determining Vintage Potential

There are beer cellars out there with hundreds and hundreds of bottles that, in the end, turn out to be nothing more than beer cemeteries, places where once-delicious brews went to die. But I've also seen cellars with only 20 or 30 bottles that nevertheless yield incredibly rewarding beers. It's not how many bottles you put in your cellar that counts but how well you choose them — how much knowledge of each beer's aging potential you can bring to the question of whether to cellar it or drink it fresh. At the heart of every good beer cellar is an educated beer taster. The savvy cellarer doesn't just chase the latest, greatest brew, but instead spends time evaluating and understanding each beer that's going to be aged.

Tasting a beer with the aim of determining its cellar potential takes both knowledge and experience. Before you can predict how a beer is likely to age, you need to understand the various components that make up the beer. For example, knowing how a beer's estery aroma will develop depends on how much you know about esters. Once you gain some familiarity with the different parts of a beer, you will then be able to gauge how they will change during the aging process. Having this understanding enables a cellar master to separate the age-worthy brews from the beers that will fall apart with the passing of time.

The aspects of beer a taster needs to become familiar with are no great mystery and are probably recognizable to most beer enthusiasts. These components are closely linked with the different flavors, aromas, and mouthfeel of the various types of beer. My list of components, which is tailored to aged beer, is as follows:

- Malt
- Hops
- Yeast esters and phenols
- Alcohol

- Wood (if present)
- Oxidation
- Microbiota (if present)

Once you have an understanding of each of these components, you also have a framework for evaluating any particular beer and determining if it deserves a spot in your cellar. You'll find that a few styles traditionally lend themselves to aging based on their makeup, but it's still important to critique each beer in terms of its individual components. One of the most elegant aging beers of all time is the classic Flanders red ale, but if you've ever had the misfortune of trying a vintage bottle from a subpar brewer, you'll know that you end up with a bottle of pricey malt vinegar. But I'm getting ahead of myself; first, let's break down each characteristic and look at how it can be expected to change as it ages.

Barley is the grain typically malted for the making of beer.

MALT

As grapes are to wine, so malt is to beer. Malt is the base, the very heart of beer, responsible not only for the dominant taste but also the alcohol content. By technical definition, a malt is any grain seed that has been processed (malted) to convert its starches into sugars. In general, barley and wheat are the predominant malts used, but occasionally malts such as rye, buckwheat, or even spelt are used. Part of the malting process is called kilning, in which the grain is heated to develop those distinctive malty flavors so familiar to beer drinkers. The caramel, chocolate, or espresso flavors found in some beers come from kilning malt at higher temperatures to the point of "roasting." These malts impart color, flavor, and sweetness — all very important to an aged beer, as we'll see later.

A More Sophisticated Beverage?

Because brewers are able to manipulate grain through a multitude of malting and roasting processes, there is a far wider range of flavors in beer than in wine. Thanks to the variety of specialty malts available to brewers, beers from your average liquor store can offer flavors ranging from biscuits to toffee to espresso. If malts were as limited in beer as grapes are in wine, the only variation in beers would be from the different malt varietals. The choices on even the most expansive beer menu would offer only something like four beers: pilsner, two-row, Vienna, and Munich. Pretty boring. And wine lovers say that our drink is the simple quaff?

But our concern here is not beer's malt profile, which has already been covered elsewhere; instead, we just need to know what about malt is important in connection with aging a beer. Malt alone does not determine a beer's aging potential, but there are certain conditions that will enable malt to improve over time. I give three general rules below. (The keyword is *general*; as with everything in life, there are notable exceptions, and I will cover those later.)

MALT RULE NO. 1:
A beer's malt profile should have some degree of roastedness and/or kettle caramelization.

The roasted character of a beer, which can range from the caramel flavors of a Scottish-style ale to the intense espresso aspects of an imperial stout, is easily identified by beer drinkers. The roasted flavor comes from pigments in the malt called melanoidins, which are created by a series of complex chemical processes known as the Maillard reaction. Though fairly involved, the Maillard reaction is something everyone is empirically familiar with; it's the same process responsible for turning bread brown and flavorful when toasted. These melanoidins are produced both when the malt is roasted and during the boiling of the wort (via kettle caramelization).

The darker a malt's roast the greater its potential for aged flavors due to the increased number of melanoidins.

Melanoidins (and other Maillard products) are reductones, which consume oxygen and stabilize a beer over time. As these melanoidins age, they will eventually develop the sherry, Madeira, and amaretto flavors so vital to many vintage beers. The larger the amount of these Maillard products, the richer their associated flavors. Because of this, many darker beers age faster because these rich flavors appear at an earlier point than they do in their pale counterparts.

So, does this mean that the darker the beer the better? Not always. What's important is finding a balance between too many and too few melanoidins. You want enough to create some aged flavors and act as oxygen stabilizers, but not so much as to overwhelm the beer with these flavors.

To judge this balance, you need an idea of the amount of melanoidins in a beer. Unfortunately, this is one of the hardest aspects to ascertain and requires the taster to examine the richness of the malt and its other underlying flavors. Did the brewer use a decent amount of high kiln malts, or just add a little heavily roasted malt to an otherwise pale grain bill? The melanoidins resulting from kettle caramelization are also vital. When talking with many brewers with proven vintage-beer credentials, I consistently found that they all felt long boil times (approaching and sometimes exceeding four hours) were critical to creating a beer that would cellar well.

I should probably preface all this by pointing out that it applies to beers where a sherry, toffeelike sweetness is a desirable trait. This will typically be true for darker styles like barley wines, imperial stouts, Belgian quads, and similar styles, but perhaps not in a tripel or Belgian golden ale (Duvel).

Last, I don't want to imply that a beer without roasted malt should never be aged. Earlier I referred to Duvel as being a great aging beer. It is because the various esters and a slight sweetness have time to develop and the alcoholic bite has time to mellow. Plus, it's a bottle-conditioned beer and therefore benefits from considerably slower oxidation. All these aspects compensate for the thinning malt; however, the aging period is limited, peaking at only a few years, versus the decades that a well-built barley wine can stand up to.

Intense Roasted Flavors

Many beer lovers are particularly fond of the coffeelike, almost burnt, flavors found in many stouts. It's important to note, however, that these flavors will fade with time. This is often encountered when aging an imperial stout, which has both an intense roastiness and a high residual sweetness. After three or four years of aging, these beers taste much more like a black barley wine, with a toffee sweetness that blends with the reduced roastiness to create a flavor like dark chocolate. Bottom line: if you prefer an espresso flavor in these beers, it's best to drink them sooner (less than a year old) rather than later.

MALT RULE NO. 2:
A beer should have high amounts of residual malt sugars.

A beer's residual sugar content simply refers to the amount of sugar left behind after the yeast has completed its primary fermentation. A brewer can control this with the strain of yeast used and the mashing temperature. All yeast strains will leave behind some residual sugars, but certain strains have been cultured to retain more than others. (This is referred to as the yeast's attenuation.) Each yeast strain is also able to make only a certain amount of alcohol, so many brewers provide so much malt (sugars) that the yeast will die off before it can consume it all.

So why do residual sugars make for good beer aging? Over time, a beer's sugars are reduced via oxidation. By essentially being oxygen "sponges" these sugars reduce the amount of residual oxygen in a beer, thereby reducing a beer's oxidation potential. Oxidation will inevitably occur, however, and as these sugars are oxidized the by-products will adhere to the malt proteins, eventually causing them to fall out, thinning the beer. Residual sugars help by supplanting the thinning malt profile as well as providing a base for the new, developing sherry flavors to stand on.

Therefore, it's a good thing to have a lot of residual sugars at the beginning to allow the beer to make the journey. Think of it like a runner who eats a huge spaghetti dinner in preparation for a marathon, storing up carbs for the big race ahead.

There are a few notable exceptions to this rule, however. One is the dry Trappist quad ales of Belgium. They age well because of their high-phenolic character and large amount of melanoidins, which produce rich flavors when aged and make up for the lack of residual sugars. The other exception is the

The high residual sugars in Hair of the Dog Brewing Company's Adam helps this beer retain an impressive mouthfeel after years of aging.

crisp, lambic-style beers, whose wild yeasts act as an antioxidant and whose flavor profile is not malt-centric or hurt by a fading malt body.

How do you develop a feel for the amount of residual sugars in a beer? A good approach is to review the residual sugar levels in beer styles you are already familiar with. The Beer Judging Certification Program (BJCP) offers style guidelines at its website, www.bjcp.org. The guidelines indicate the typical final gravity, a measurement of the amount of sugar left in the finished beer. (See the table below for a list of common styles and their average final gravity.) Once you can associate a familiar style's expected final gravity with your experiences, judging the amount of residual sugar in beer begins to come fairly easily.

Table 1: Final gravity of common beer styles (in ascending order)

STYLE	AVERAGE FINAL GRAVITY (WATER = 1.000)	CLASSIC EXAMPLES
Light American lager	0.998–1.008	Coors Light
Gueuze	1.000–1.006	Cantillon Classic Gueuze
Saison	1.002–1.012	Saison Dupont
Berliner Weisse	1.003–1.006	Weihenstephan 1809
Belgian golden strong ale	1.005–1.016	Duvel
Dry stout	1.007–1.011	Guinness
German pilsner	1.008–1.013	Trumer Pils
American pale ale	1.010–1.015	Sierra Nevada Pale Ale
Doppelbock	1.016–1.024	Paulaner Salvator
Russian imperial stout	1.018–1.030	Stone Imperial Russian Stout
Scottish wee heavy	1.018–1.056	Belhaven Wee Heavy
Eisbock	1.020–1.035	Kulmbacher Eisbock

Final Gravity

Final gravity is the best indicator of a beer's residual sugar content. Technically, it is a measure of a beer's density when compared with that of water. The amount of sugars in a beer increases its density, so the more sugars there are, the denser the liquid. The density of water is set at 1.000, so a beer with a final gravity higher than that (say a pale ale at 1.010) has more sugar than water. Much confusion comes from beers that have final gravities that sit right at 1.000 or lower. Although these beers still have a minimal amount of unfermented sugar, the amount of alcohol (which is less dense than water) exceeds the influence of the sugar, leading to an overall density less than that of water.

MALT RULE NO. 3:
A beer should be brewed with high-quality malt.

As the saying goes, "Garbage in, garbage out." It therefore makes sense that a cellared beer should be made with the best ingredients. The challenge is knowing what makes a malt high quality and if the brewer used it or not. The first part, knowing what makes a malt of high quality, is a fairly complex endeavor. As previously discussed, there are certain malts that, because of a higher curing temperature, undergo significant Maillard reactions and therefore have a greater amount of melanoidins. The classic Vienna and Munich malts, used to create the rich bocks of Germany, are known for this. There are also malts that have low lipid (fatty acids found in some malts) levels, which makes them much less susceptible to oxidation and so enables the beer to have a longer cellar life. For these and other reasons, the pricey Maris Otter malt makes extremely rich, long-lasting beers that stand up remarkably well in the cellar.

However, although some malt varieties are better than others, much of a beer's aging potential comes down to the maltster who sources and malts the barley. If the maltster takes shortcuts or buys old or poor-quality barley, the finished product will suffer. It is up to the brewer to determine whether the malt is high quality and appropriate for the beer. Making the right choice often results in higher cost, but a forward-thinking brewer sees it as a worthwhile investment.

Knowing whether the brewer used quality malt or not is even more difficult to verify. As a taster, knowing the malt variety of the beer you're drinking is a highly developed skill that comes from extensive experience either brewing or judging beer. Still, even if you can't determine the malt used, knowing how crucial high-quality malt is at least enables you to understand why some beers will age better than others, and why paying a higher up-front cost for a quality product can be worth the investment.

HOPS

Hops were initially used in beer to extend shelf life. The brewing conditions prior to the advent of the chemical sanitizers used today essentially ensured that a beer would start to show signs of contamination at some point. It was discovered that hops slowed the spoiling, besides adding flavors and aromas that were complementary to beer's malty sweetness.

The preserving effect of hops comes primarily from the acids extracted from the hop cones when they are boiled. As every beer lover knows, extra hops were added to the ales sent over from England to the British troops stationed in India to help the ale survive the long journey, earning this hoppy English ale the name India Pale Ale. Likewise, Bavaria, in an effort to ensure the quality of its duchy's beer over surrounding areas, enacted the famous (or infamous) *Reinheitsgebot* law in 1516, which required all its beers to be produced with hops in addition to barley and water. The law was adopted by Germany in 1871 when Bavaria became part of the nation.

Considering the strict sanitation controls in the modern brewing industry and the repeal of the *Reinheitsgebot* in 1988, using hops for their preservative characteristic has become more of a historical footnote; their main value nowadays is for the bitterness, flavors, and aromas they impart to a beer.

The Hallertau hop has a high beta-to-alpha-acid ratio.

So, since hops have antibacterial value, are they beneficial in terms of aging beer? Unfortunately, no, since hop presence simply fades over time. And the distinctive flavors and aromas from those delightful little cones are too fleeting to put up with much of a stint in the cellar. This is important to keep in mind, because as the hoppy aspects disappear, the beer that remains is often quite unbalanced. Therefore, beers that are hop-centric (for example, IPAs) are typically not good candidates for aging.

Hop Alpha and Beta Acids and Isomerization

The active ingredient in hops is the resin lupulin, which comes from the female (cone) part of the *Humulus lupus* plant. Lupulin contains what are called alpha and beta acids, as well as some essential oils. As the hops are boiled, the alpha acids undergo a process called isomerization, which gives beer much of its unique hoppy bitterness. These iso-alpha acids are very susceptible to oxidation, and over time their bitterness will disappear and leave behind a stale flavor. The beta acids, on the other hand, do not isomerize during the boil, and therefore do not initially contribute any flavor to the beer. With age, though (in dry storage or in the brewed beer), the beta acids oxidize into compounds called hulupones, which contribute a bitterness similar to the iso-alpha acids. Unlike the alpha acids, hulupones are stable, maintaining their bitterness in the cellar and helping a beer retain balance over time.

The fact that hops fade with time is widely known. It's one of the changes easy to note in an older beer, and the brewing industry has done a fairly respectable job of alerting customers to the fact. The head brewer at Russian River Brewing Company, Vinnie Cilurzo, has gone so far as to plaster the label of its double IPA, Pliny the Elder, with warnings like SIT ON EGGS, DON'T SIT ON PLINY, or HOPS DON'T IMPROVE WITH AGE.

When evaluating a beer for aging, try to imagine what it would taste and smell like without its various hop components. It takes a while to develop this skill, but it's an essential one. A good way to acquire it is to find a six-month-old IPA (check some strip-mall liquor store with a dusty collection of craft brews) and taste it side by side with a fresh version. The hop differences should be noticeable, while the malt changes should be fairly minimal, helping greatly to showcase the hop degradation.

As a beer ages, the hop-derived compounds go through a degradation process that eliminates much of their associated bitterness, flavor, and aroma. This degradation is due mostly to oxidation from the oxygen that is inadvertently introduced into the beer during various brewhouse processes. The alpha acids, especially the isomerized (bitter) ones, are much more susceptible to degradation, and as they break down, a multitude of compounds are created, most notably trans-2-nonenal, which produces the dreaded wet-cardboard flavor. (See the box below for more about this.) Therefore, be especially alert to the hop character when considering whether or not to age a beer. Cellaring can not only cause it to lose a vital component of its taste profile but also create negative new flavors.

Trans-2-Nonenal

Of all the off flavors possible in an aged beer (and there are a lot), the one associated with trans-2-nonenal is among the worst, and definitely the most prevalent. People often describe it as something like "sucking on a piece of cardboard." I say "something like" because it's a flavor many people initially struggle to name, myself included. It wasn't until I was at a beer tasting, and a seasoned BJCP judge mentioned that the Belhaven 80 Scottish ale was "riddled with cardboard," that I could finally identify the taste. Once I realized that *that* was the infamous cardboard flavor, I was surprised by how familiar I was with it: it's that unmistakeable stale, old flavor. Until then, I would never have called it cardboard, but when I thought about it, I decided I couldn't think of a better way to describe it and have grudgingly stuck with it ever since.

A hop's beta acids, on the other hand, degrade much more slowly, allowing an aged beer to retain its bitterness longer. On top of that, as these acids do degrade, various esters can arise that give a beer fruity, winelike, or musty flavor, and also greater complexity.

While the hop's beta and alpha acids provide bitterness, it's the hop oils that provide hoppy flavor and aroma. As a beer ferments and ages, these oils undergo a multitude of complex chemical reactions that are still not well understood. What we do know is that, due to oxidation, these flavors and aromas will disappear over time, with the myrcene oil-derived aspects (citrus, floral) being the first to go.

So put yourself in the shoes of a brewer who is designing a beer to age. You would want a hop varietal that has a high ratio of beta-to-alpha acids, which will reduce the trans-2-nonenal potential while retaining the beta acid's bitterness through the aging process. Luckily, there are hop varietals that meet the need, and, no big surprise, they are used in beers that age well, like English barley wines and Belgian quads. Notable varietals are hops of the noble and English varieties, which sometimes reach close to a 1:1 alpha-to-beta-acid ratio.

Table 2: Common hop varietals and their average alpha and beta acid content

VARIETAL	ALPHA ACID PERCENT	BETA ACID PERCENT
Hallertau	3–5	4–5
Mount Hood	6–8	5–7
Saaz	3–4	3–4
Tettnanger	4–5	3–5
Fuggle	5–6	2–3
Styrian Golding	4–8	2–5
Willamette	6–7	4–5
Cascade	6–8	4–7
Centennial	10–13	4–5
Nugget	12–14	4–6
Simcoe	12–14	4–5
Summit	17–19	4–5

When evaluating the hop profile of a beer, consider the varietal(s) the brewer used. Sometimes this information can be found on the bottle or at the brewer's website. The other approach is to use your nose. Most beer lovers know what American hops smell and taste like: just think of that citrusy, resiny goodness in your favorite IPA. While great in a fresh brew, that smell can be a warning sign when thinking about cellaring, since American hops usually have a very high alpha-to-beta-acid ratio. Proceed with caution.

HOPS IN BARLEY WINES AND STOUTS

All right, so don't age IPAs or double IPAs long term, but what about the hop-heavy American barley wines and imperial stouts? If you look at their IBU ratings, which are an indication of the amount of hop bitterness (think alpha acids), these beers can rival a double IPA for bitterness. But all the marketing and buzz out there says these are made to cellar. For me, they have to be carefully evaluated to determine how long they can realistically be expected to improve. Did the brewer plan for some hop degradation when choosing the malts and yeast, or use a hop varietal high in beta acids that will stand up to cellaring? How dominant are the hoppy flavors and aromas?

Experience has shown me that many of these uber-hopped barley wines and imperial stouts can benefit from a year of aging. Although the vibrant, fresh hop flavors will be somewhat muted, a year helps mellow the alcohol and produce some slight aged malt and esters. More than that, though, and cardboard flavors can start to creep in because of the big amount of high-alpha-acid hops. But there are wonderful exceptions: you need look no further than the deliciousness of a 10-year-old bottle of Sierra Nevada's hoppy barley wine Bigfoot to find one. Breweries that exercise extreme caution against oxygen pickup can produce beers quite resistant to hop-induced trans-2-nonenal. With brewing processes improving every day, look for many big hoppy beers that will stand up well to longer and longer times in the cellar.

YEAST ESTERS AND PHENOLS

Yeast is the catalyst that gets everything moving in a beer. It's the workhorse that takes the thick, viscous wort (unfermented beer) and transforms it into beer. Generally, yeast can be classified into two categories: ale and lager yeasts. (The wild yeast *Brettanomyces*, and the bacteria that are often pitched

The double IPA Heady Topper, from The Alchemist, and Big Sky's Olde Bluehair Barley Wine both have a hop bitterness of 75 IBUs.

with it, *Pediococcus* and *Lactobacillus*, fall into their own category and are covered in the Microbiota subsection on page 49.)

There are many differences between ale yeast and lager yeast. The most mentioned (but least important, in my opinion) is that ale yeast sits at the top of the wort during fermentation while lager yeast prefers to do its magic on the bottom. To me, where fermentation occurs is not important, but rather, what flavors and aromas result from it.

The next difference between the two yeasts is that of fermentation temperature. Lager yeast prefers the temperature of the caves they were first cultured in, 45 to 55 °F (7–13°C). Ale yeast is most comfortable at temperatures warmer than that, say 65 to 75°F (18–24°C).

Experience tells us that beers age well at or below their fermentation temperature. This is related to a chemistry concept called activation temperature. Activation temperature is nothing more than the specific temperature required for a particular chemical reaction to occur. So, if a brewer uses an ale yeast strain, the activation temperature for primary fermentation to occur would be 65°F/18°C (or thereabouts depending on the strain). While everyone is aware of the main chemical process in beer, the conversion of sugars to alcohol through fermentation, there are hundreds of other chemical processes that can, and do, occur depending on temperature. Many of them will not produce a noticeable difference in a beer, but the ones that do may leave off-tastes that the brewer never intended and you won't want in your beer.

> **Yeast is the catalyst that gets everything moving in a beer.**

That's why it's best to cellar beer at or below the fermentation temperature (your best guess, at least) so as to avoid starting any chemical processes that have not occurred up to this point. Ales are often better candidates for aging because of the versatility of the cellar-temperature range.

The most important difference between ale yeast and lager yeast, however, concerns the production and/or metabolism of fermentation byproducts. Due largely to fermentation temperature, ale yeast generates a multitude of yeast esters, fusel alcohols (more on these a little later), and sometimes phenols. Lager yeasts, on the other hand, generally produce very low amounts of these, thereby giving their beers a clean taste that showcases the malt and hop aspects of the beer. As a result, lagers often don't age well because as the hops fade, the beer is left with only the malt flavors, which become sherrylike, caramelly, and one-dimensional.

The esters produced by ale yeasts vary widely, but in general they can be described as fruity. The classic bubblegum and banana flavors found in hefeweizens are esters that are a key component of the signature yeast used for brewing this style. Esters age much like a fruit does, meaning while a fresh beer might have esters suggesting pears, peaches, or apples, its aged version could bring to mind dried figs, raisins, or prunes. Keep in mind too that esters can come from components other than primary fermentation by-products, like when hop beta acids degrade to form the fruity, winelike methyl-butyrate ester.

What Are Esters?

The vast majority of fruits owe their distinctive aroma to chemical compounds called esters (which is why yeast-derived esters in beer typically smell so fruity). Esters are typically created when an alcohol and an acid combine. In fruit, they come from the inherently abundant acids and the alcohols that are a by-product of cell metabolism. Although there may be many different esters in a single fruit, each variety seems to have one characteristic ester that provides its distinctive aroma. In apples, ethyl alcohol and acetic acid combine to form ethyl acetate. In pears, hexyl alcohol (a higher alcohol) combines with acetic acid to make hexyl acetate. Another characteristic flavor often encountered in beers (German Weissbier in particular) is isoamyl acetate, which comes from the combination of isoamyl alcohol and acetic acid. This is the ester in bananas that gives them their distinctive smell, and it is especially susceptible to quick degradation from oxidation.

Because they add a richness and complexity complementing the sweet malt flavors and aromas, aged yeast esters are a highly desired component of classic vintage beer styles such as barley wine, Flanders brown ale, and imperial stout. Look for beers of these styles to have a decent ester presence when fresh to ensure that the aged version will have the dried-fruit flavors that make them worth aging.

Besides esters, phenols are another potential by-product of ale yeast. Typically, phenols aren't a desired component of an ale and usually indicate poor brewing sanitation. But, there are a few styles, notably Belgian ales and

The distinctive flavor note of a German hefeweizen and the aroma of a fresh banana come from the same chemical compound, isoamyl acetate.

German wheat beers, that have smoky, clovelike, or peppery components that come from yeast-derived phenols.

As phenols age, their flavors typically take drastic turns. The clove and pepper phenols tend to evolve into a sweet, vanilla presence, while smoky phenols (which can also come from smoked malts) develop tobacco or leather notes. In the best cases, these new flavors bring a rich complexity to an aged beer; Schneider's Aventinus, a German wheat doppelbock, is an excellent example of this. Other times, however, beers can be left unbalanced once their original phenolic flavors, so crucial to their overall balance, have transformed.

ALCOHOL

As the yeast tucks into the wort's cornucopia of fermentable sugars, it creates alcohol. The primary alcohol derived from this process is ethyl alcohol, but other types, called fusel, or higher, alcohols can also be created. These alcohols have a variety of flavors and aromas and are responsible for the spicy, warming, prickly sensations you can pick out of strong beer. While undesirable in lagers, a low level of fusels can sometimes add depth to ales, bringing out fruity, amaretto, or wine aspects, especially when aged. In a fresh beer, though, they're usually a negative attribute, imparting a boozy character or a solvent-like taste.

Booziness in a beer is often a good justification for aging. Given time, the booziness will mellow and fade, creating a more drinkable beer. This change results from the maturing of higher alcohols, which are simply ethyl-alcohol molecules with additional atoms attached. As this happens, new flavors and aromas are created, including aldehydes, the chemical compounds responsible for the sweet toffee and almond flavors so desired in many aged beers.

In addition to aldehydes, new and distinctive esters are also created as the fusels age. These esters occur when higher alcohols combine with various acids in the beer (notably aging hop beta acids) and typically produce fruity, winelike flavors that, when combined with the matured chocolate flavors in aged stouts, create a delicious black-cherry note. They can also result in distinctive portlike flavors when combined with the sherry aspects of aged malt melanoidins.

So don't immediately be put off by a strong, boozy nose when evaluating a beer for aging. In fact, as long as there's some roasted-malt melanoidins to complement, this is a good indicator of a beer's aging potential. Anybody who has tasted a young Thomas Hardy's Ale can attest to the "hotness" of the beer; however, when aged, this beer is considered one of the best vintage beers ever brewed. Similar to most cellar-worthy wines, many beers that improve with age suffer through an awkward adolescence.

Time Is Money

Though fusel alcohols are vital to an aged beer's long-term character, they are not prevalent in many American beers produced today. This is due mainly to the very quick bottle-to-market nature of the American brewing industry. As the saying goes, "Time is money," and many breweries are not willing to tie up valuable square footage with beers that need time to mellow their booziness. English barley wines, on the other hand, were traditionally made with a high fusel nose and then aged on-site for long periods to allow the beer to mature. George Gale's Prize Old Ale, considered one of the best aging English barley wines ever brewed, was aged for a minimum of two years on-site prior to release. (Perhaps not surprisingly, the brewery was forced to sell in 2005 to rival brewery Fuller's because of "the rising cost of doing business.") This difference means that while many cellarers find that old English strong ales develop intense complexities, many of the American incarnations are a bit simpler when mature.

In addition to the presence of higher alcohols, the overall percentage of alcohol in a beer is important as to how well it will age (of utmost importance, really). It is fairly well known that for a beer to last a long time in the cellar, it should be high in alcohol. Why this is so, however, is not easy to answer. Alcohol has a variety of highly complex effects on the chemical

The strong initial booziness of Thomas Hardy's Ale mellows into complex, sweet, fruit notes.

THOMAS
HARDY'S ALE

In "The Trumpet-Major" Hardy wrote of Dorchester's strong beer "It was of the most beautiful colour that the eye of an artist in beer could desire; full in body, yet brisk as a volcano; piquant, yet without a twang; luminous as an autumn sunset; free from streakiness of taste changes in an aging beer. Nevertheless, in simple, general terms, alcohol can be seen to act as a preservative. The more alcohol present, the slower all those chemical reactions will be. As the old adage goes, "Good things come to those who wait," and the positive flavors that can be found in vintage beer (figs, port, toffee, and many others) come from slow, stubborn processes that cannot be rushed. By slowing things down, you're buying time to enable the creation of these flavors, a key to successful beer aging.

A good analogy for understanding this process might be to compare the aging of a high-gravity beer with cooking a pot roast. Most likely you've heard the culinary advice "slow and low" in reference to the optimal way to cook roasts, stews, and similar dishes. Rush a beef pot roast at 400°F (205°C), and you end up with a dry, chewy piece of meat, but cook that same roast nice and slow at 250°F (121°C), and you'll be rewarded with a melt-in-your-mouth tender, richly flavored dish. The slow roasting is key because it gives time for the connective tissue, called collagen, to break down and gelatinize, which is what gives the dish its looked-for richness and succulence. However, since this gelatinization occurs at a slow rate, the roast needs to be cooked at a low enough temperature to allow time for this reaction to occur. This slow roasting also gives the dish's spices and juices a chance to integrate and create complex flavors.

Following my analogy, just as a slow cooking is good for the pot roast, a slow aging is good for the aged beer; to maintain a slow roasting, you need a low temperature, and to sustain a long aging, you need a high alcohol content. The important flavor work collagen does in a roast is comparable

Goose Island's Bourbon County Stout weighs in at a hefty 14.5 percent ABV, permitting very slow development.

to the melanoidins, esters, and other compounds that go into making a great-tasting aged beer, and just as you can't rush collagen, you can't hurry the slow processes in beer aging that produce great flavors in cellared beer.

Why Do Strong Beers Leave "Legs" on My Glass?

Astute beer tasters may notice that as they swirl a particularly strong beer in their snifter, long, thin films of liquid appear on the sides of their glass. These are commonly known as "tears" or "legs" and come from the evaporation of alcohol. When beer spreads out on the surface of a glass during swirling, it evaporates because of the increased surface area exposed to air. Since alcohol lowers the attraction between molecules, as it evaporates, the water is increasingly attracted to the glass surface and actually pulls itself up onto it. Eventually this water "climb" succumbs to gravity and falls in the form of a droplet, or "tear."

A strong beer like a barley wine can leave "legs" on a glass.

WOOD

Initially, wooden barrels were used by brewers simply as a vessel in which to store their product. Back then, the intricate flavors that a barrel imparts to a beer were not a factor in their use, and were, in fact, rarely desired. Many breweries actually lined their barrels with pine pitch to prevent a transfer of flavors. Over time, the high demands in skill and time required to make wooden barrels gave way to the industrial manufacture of the stainless steel tanks seen in the brewing industry today. So, although wooden barrels are no longer cost-efficient for storing beer, many brewers have discovered that aging certain beers in wooden casks adds a host of complementary flavors and thus a deeper complexity.

Primary Fermentation vs. Barrel Aging

Although many brewers use oak vessels for secondary aging or conditioning, they rarely use them for primary fermentation. There are a few exceptions, however, and this process can add some unexpected subtleties to a beer. The Firestone Walker Brewing Company of Paso Robles, California, uses oak for primary fermentation in a few of its brews, most notably the DBA (Double Barrel Ale). When the compounds derived from the active yeast mesh with the oak, furfurylthiol, a sulfur-containing chemical, is created, giving the beer a distinct aroma identified with roasting coffee.

Though a variety of woods have been used over the years — redwood, cedar, and chestnut, to name a few — oak barrels were favored because of their pliable nature, making them particularly watertight. Nowadays, oak is also preferred for the distinct flavors it adds to a beer. Most of these flavors come from the tannic compounds in the wood, such as vanillin (vanilla), lactones (peach, coconut), eugenol (clove), and guaiacol (cinnamon). The extracting qualities of alcohol pull these flavors out of the barrels to become part of the finished product.

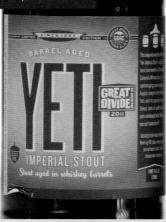

Great Divide makes both an oak-aged and a barrel-aged version of Yeti, its imperial stout.

Barrel Aging vs. Oak Aging

"The devil is in the details." It's often the case that a beer labeled "oak aged" isn't in fact aged in an oak barrel. Because of the cost and logistics that come with accommodating large barrels in an already crowded brewery, many brewers opt instead to add oak chips to their stainless steel fermentation tanks. These chips look a lot like the wood chips you see in the grocery store that are used in barbecue smokers. While this method has its obvious advantages, such "oaked" beers lack the depth of a beer that has had a good rest in an actual barrel. This is partly because barrels are made from the oak heartwood, or center of the tree, which is particularly rich in the absorptive lignins, whereas the chips can be made from any part of the tree. But it's mostly due to the porosity of barrels, which allows beers aged in barrels to become slightly oxidized, creating complementary aging-derived flavors. When forking out big bucks for an oak-aged beer, be sure to look for labels that say "barrel aged" or give another clear indication that an actual barrel was used.

For the most part, oak is highly insoluble, which is why the barrels don't leak. However, there is a small soluble component of the wood, lignin, that will absorb stored liquid. When the beer is drawn into the lignin, the alcohol extracts the oaky flavors distinctive in a barrel-aged beer. Because of this, low-alcohol beers (under 7 percent ABV) are typically not aged in barrels because of their lack of extracting capabilities.

In addition to the commonly seen wine and whiskey barrels, brewers occasionally use barrels in which cognac, sherry, rum, or other alcohols have been stored. Each type of barrel will have absorbed some amount of the spirit or wine that it previously stored. When filled with beer, the wood absorbs some of it and expels a portion of the wine or spirit it was previously holding, lending yet another layer of complexity to the beer.

Oak-derived flavors stay fairly stable throughout the aging process. This should come as no surprise, considering that they come from a tree as strong and long-lived as an old oak. As the malt, yeast, and hop flavors go on a roller-coaster ride, the oak flavors remain comparatively stable. Nonetheless, studies have shown that the vanilla, coconut, and clove flavors are somewhat susceptible to oxygen and eventually fade, vanilla being the first to go. The cinnamon flavor from the guaiacol has actually been shown to increase over time.

Whether the relative stability of oak flavors is a good or bad thing is up to the cellarer. More often than not, the oak will complement the newly derived flavors in an aged beer, but sometimes, and particularly in connection with the developing caramel malt flavors, it can combine to create a cloying sweetness that is overwhelming in a beer. The fact that it remains constant, though, helps to make it one of the easier components to evaluate when determining the cellar potential of a beer.

One final, important thing to consider when determining the cellar potential of a barrel-aged beer is that of oxidation. Barrels, unlike glass bottles, are porous and allow a very small amount of oxygen to pass through to their liquid. This additional oxygen increases oxidation-based developments in the beer. You will often find that a beer that has spent an extended amount of time in a barrel has developed aging characteristics much further advanced than those of their counterparts of the same vintage that have not been oak aged. So, be careful when cellaring barrel-aged beers that it's not for too long, since it has already undergone oxidation at an advanced rate.

Virgin Barrels

Occasionally, and only very occasionally, breweries will invest in fresh, or "virgin," oak barrels to age their beers in. Odell Brewing Company's Woodcut series, a succession of varying beer styles aged in virgin oak barrels, is a notable example of this. Woodcut No. 1, an old ale, shocked the beer world when it debuted at $25 a bottle. However, consider that the series is now at No. 7 and counting: there is obviously a market segment that appreciates the nuances of fresh oak barrels. As a fan myself, I hope more breweries will feel compelled to follow suit.

OXIDATION

Just about any publication that bothers to say anything on the topic of aging beer will warn readers of the danger and detriment of oxidized beer and its "cardboard, stale" flavors. While this can certainly be the result in many situations, such critics, the same ones who dismiss beer aging as an odd European fascination, overlook the incredibly wonderful flavors and aromas that can be derived from the oxidation of a properly selected beer. At its worst, oxidation can create trans-2-nonenal and harsh, degraded phenolic compounds, but it's also capable of producing an amazing diversity of

Woodcut No. 5 is a Belgian quad aged in virgin-oak barrels.

flavors like dried fruit, toffee, port, and hazelnut. Reactive oxygen species (ROS), the molecules that cause oxidation, are present to some degree in all beers and are responsible for an array of reactions and flavors as a beer ages. Therefore, unlike wine, which has a mass of antioxidants (derived from grape skins) to quell the ROS, oxidation is an inevitable process in beer, and it must be taken into account when considering aging potential. Understanding the process is quite simple: oxidation is just the loss of an electron from an oxygen-based molecule to another molecule. The molecule that loses an electron is an ROS, or has been "oxidized." It's when that lost electron transfers to another molecule that things get a little complicated and a whole host of varying flavors and aromas are affected.

Size Really Does Matter

Wine buffs have long known that 1.5L magnums age more slowly than their 750mL counterparts. Much of the difference is due to the amount of oxygen picked up during bottling. Because most bottling-derived oxygen is introduced during the initial filling movement, a large bottle absorbs about the same amount as a small one. Additionally, the head space (and its associated oxygen) is about the same in both small and large bottles. The larger liquid-to-oxygen ratio in the bigger bottles allows the contents to better deal with the oxidation over time. Furthermore, the larger mass (glass and liquid) makes the beer (or wine) less susceptible to temperature swings, encouraging smooth, steady aging. Vintage kegs age especially slowly (and well) for these reasons. For example, just because that keg of '95 Bigfoot was awesome, don't assume that a 12-ounce bottle of '95 will drink the same.

Oxidation does mainly four things in a beer: creates a variety of new compounds with the kilned malt molecules; degrades the alpha acids left by the hops; causes the esters and phenols produced by the yeast during fermentation to develop in flavor and aroma; and forms aldehydes from higher alcohols. Let's take up each one in detail.

OXIDATION EFFECT NO. 1:
Kilned Malt Oxidation

The oxidation of malt can have both positive and negative aspects to it. The inherent oxygen in a beer can either oxidize the malt's fatty acids to create the stale-tasting, trans-2-nonenal compound, or it can react with the melanoidins to create sherry and portlike flavors. Studies show that temperature makes a big difference in the direction the malt oxidation takes. One showed that a sample beer aged at 86°F (30°C) had a predominantly cardboard flavor, while the same beer aged at 68°F (30°C) produced mostly sweet, caramel flavors. Most likely, aging will not create just one or the other of these two tastes, but in any beer deemed worthy of aging, the melanoidin component should win out handily.

In addition to temperature, alcohol content affects malt oxidation. Alcohol slows the malt oxidation process, allowing the positive, sherry flavors plenty of time to develop. Since melanoidins take time to oxidize, this lengthened window is critical to a properly aged beer. Again, much like that perfectly cooked pot roast, slow and low is truly the best way to develop well-aged malt flavors and aromatics.

OXIDATION EFFECT NO. 2:
Hop Alpha Acid Degradation

Unlike with malts, the oxidation of hops is decidedly negative. The ROS break down the isomerized alpha acids, which leaves the beer unbalanced and potentially with a variety of off-tastes. As in the malt process, high alcohol content helps slow the degradation of the hops' bitterness and enables their flavors and aromas to last longer.

In contrast to the alpha acids, however, the bitterness from the hop beta acids (hulupones) is more resilient. Additionally, the hop components eventually convert to methyl butyrate, which lends many vintage beers a wine-like aspect. When combined with the new, caramel flavors made by the aldehydes, this wine note achieves a flavor somewhere between port and candied pineapple.

OXIDATION EFFECT NO. 3:
Yeast Ester Development

A third major effect of oxidation is the transformation of the yeast esters' flavor profile. As these components age, they become more volatile, giving aged beers a more intense, complex aroma. And while yeast esters in an unaged beer are often reminiscent of fresh fruit, the yeast esters in an aged beer are more akin to dried or candied fruit. A good way to tell how the esters' flavors and aromas will change over time is to compare them with how these aspects in fresh fruit change when they're dried.

When fruit dries as the water evaporates from its flesh, the acids become more concentrated, and this creates additional alcohols, two of which combine to form an intense amount of the fruit's characteristic ester. In addition, as fruit dries, a browning enzyme oxidation reaction (caused by the elevated heat) occurs between the sugars and amino acids. The result of the browning reaction is the creation of caramel-like flavors. These caramel and fruit

A vintage beer might feature the aroma of any of a wide range of dried fruits.

flavors merge to form the tastes and aromas distinctive of raisins, figs, dates, and prunes.

Knowing what happens to give dried fruits their characteristic flavors helps explain why similar tastes and aromas arise in a vintage beer. The added fruity esters created in the bottle during aging combine with the already-present esters to produce a powerfully fruity profile. When these esters join with the aldehyde-based caramel flavors, the taste experience is remarkably similar to that with dried fruit.

OXIDATION EFFECT NO. 4:
Aldehyde Creation from Fusels

The higher alcohols common to many high-gravity beers oxidize over time to create aldehydes. These aldehydes produce a variety of flavors and aromas but in general are sweet — amaretto, toffee, caramel, bread pudding, and treacle frequently come to mind. They thus contribute attractive aspects to an aged beer's flavor profile. The fusel alcohol's initial flavors are harsh and prickly, leaving the unpleasant taste of solvent — another good reason to age beer.

All that being said, keep in mind that the benefits of oxidation have a very definite ceiling. In time, the various positive aspects from oxidation will be destroyed, degraded by the same process that created them. Ask brewers if they would ever intentionally oxidize a beer to try to accelerate or accentuate the aging characteristics, and most respond with an emphatic "No." You might think this is a ludicrous question to begin with, but that's exactly what's done in the port and sherry industries. However, because of their much higher alcohol content (usually 20 percent, almost twice that of your average barley wine) from fortification with distilled spirits, these beverages are much better suited to deal with the oxidative process than beer. The general consensus is that enough oxygen is introduced during the brewing process to develop sufficient oxidation-derived characteristics.

Put a Cork In It?

A bottle's closure type can affect its aging rate. Corks let minute amounts of oxygen through over time, something widely acknowledged in the wine world. However, wine is unpressurized and therefore more affected by this seepage. (To a point, beer's internal carbonation pressure keeps oxygen out.) The tight-fitting nature of caps makes them the superior closure type when considering oxidation, though the older twist-off varieties are a definite exception due to threading leakage. Watch out for the rubber o-rings of swing-tops; they are especially prone to oxygen introduction over long periods of time.

MICROBIOTA

The term *microbiota* refers to the living microscopic organisms in a beer. In 99 percent of all beers, the only microbiota the brewer wants present is the traditional beer yeast, *Saccharomyces cerevisiae*. In many larger breweries, a beer is pasteurized before it's bottled to prevent the growth of spoilage-causing microorganisms and stabilize the short-term flavor profile. During pasteurization, the beer is heated to a high enough temperature to kill the yeast and inactivate many of the enzymes in the beer. While this achieves the aim of preventing bacterial spoilage, the heat exposure also increases the rate of chemical changes in beer and kills the oxygen-consuming yeast, an obvious detriment to any beer being laid down for aging.

As a compromise, most breweries filter their beer instead of subjecting it to the harsh pasteurization process. With filtering, much of the yeast and potentially damaging microorganisms are removed. This produces a beer not quite as sterile as a pasteurized one and with a much better aging outlook than one that has been heated. Still, although filtration skirts the problem of too much heat and leaves some yeast behind, it also takes away some of the flavor and aroma components, even body, of a beer.

Some breweries even add additional sugar to a beer prior to bottling to respark fermentation in the bottle. Such "bottle-conditioned" beers, as

The live yeast in bottle-conditioned ales consumes residual oxygen and thus slows oxidation.

they're called, and really any beer containing living yeast, have the potential for much better flavor development over time because they're dynamic, living products able to consume oxygen and create, absorb, and mellow flavors. Therefore, while there is a certain intrinsic risk that the beer will become contaminated, it's one that most cellarers will gladly take in exchange for the greater depth of flavor possible in an aged beer.

Over time, the live yeast in a beer will succumb to autolysis. Essentially self-destruction, autolysis occurs when the cell walls of yeast break down, dispensing their contents into the beer. In an aging beer, this typically results from the high-alcohol environment of the beer, though it can also be caused by high carbonation. The flavors produced by autolysis range fairly widely. When combined with the high acidity of dark malts, these flavors often suggest rust, ink, or even soy sauce, which essentially ruins many aged imperial stouts. In brown-colored ales, it's possible to get a meaty, so-called umami flavor, which has the potential to add some complexity to a well-aged beer. In very light ales (such as a gueuze), autolysis can give rise to a *sur lie* effect, that prized, toasty, hazelnut flavor found in aged Champagne. Autolysis characteristics typically show up only after long periods of aging, with the acidic imperial stouts (from the roasted malts) and sour ales being the first to display them, around the five-year mark.

Is This Beer Alive?

It's often hard to tell if a beer has been pasteurized. American consumers have shown little interest in the question, so breweries usually don't bother to indicate whether their beer contains live yeast. (For British beer drinkers' take on the issue, see CAMRA's [Campaign for Real Ale] website, www.camra.org.uk.) Without a label indication, the best way to determine this is to look for the telltale yeast cake in the bottom of the bottle. Otherwise, you can always e-mail the brewery and ask. Breweries that don't pasteurize are usually very happy to brag about the fact.

Asking people in the beer industry whether they would age a beer that doesn't contain live yeast garners a wide range of responses. Many say there's no point because the beer will only degrade after being stripped of all its dynamic, oxygen-consuming yeast. Others, including myself, consider that while not optimal, there's still cellar potential in a carefully selected, pasteurized beer; it just may succumb to aging faster. Plus, along with the yeast, the autolysis concerns are eliminated.

The other microbiota found in the remaining 1 percent of beers (actually, probably more like 0.1 percent) are the little organisms that contribute to making a "wild" or "sour" beer. The aging of these beers is very complex. Ask some of the famed lambic blenders of Belgium's Senne Valley how their beers age, and every one of them will give you a different answer. What is known, however, is that most sour beers become more integrated with time as their stronger flavors mellow to match some of the more subtle ones. A cellarer's best hope of estimating how a sour beer will develop, and whether it will continue to improve, is understanding the unusual microbiota and their by-products that give these beers their characteristic flavors and bouquet.

To gain a better understanding of sour beers, a good place to start is with the aforementioned lambic beers of Belgium. Following is an overview of the ongoing dynamics of aging lambics. If you're interested in furthering your knowledge of the subject, I recommend Jeff Sparrow's classic book, *Wild Brews*.

Lambic beers have many different microbes because of their "open" fermented nature; meaning that instead of the freshly brewed wort going into a sealed stainless steel tank, the wort is run out into large, flat copper pans (called *koelschip* in Flemish) that are exposed to the air. Countless bacteria and yeasts drop from the air into the sticky, sweet wort and set to work. Once the brewer decides it has been sufficiently inoculated, it is transferred into large wooden casks to ferment. These casks are usually quite old and contribute a good dose of their own microbes left behind from previous batches.

This large copper koelschip was used for open fermentation at the De Dolle Brewery in Belgium.

IN ILLA BRETTANOMYCES, NOS FIDES

Above the entryway to The Lost Abbey's barrel-aging room is a notice that translates roughly as "In the Wild Yeast We Believe."

Of the multitude of microscopic "bugs" (as they're often referred to in the brewing industry) present in a fermenting lambic, the ones that especially affect the taste profile are the acid-producing bacteria, *Lactobacillus*, *Pediococcus*, and *Acetobacter*, and the yeast *Brettanomyces*. The traditional beer yeast, *Saccharomyces*, is also present and produces its own alcohols, esters, and phenols as well. These different microbes provide various aspects crucial to the overall character of the beer.

Pediococcus (also called "pedio" for short) and *Lactobacillus* ("lacto") create lactic acid, which gives lambic its characteristic sour taste. This taste shouldn't be confused with a vinegar kind of sourness, which comes from acetic acid. Lactic acid produces a flavor best likened to unsweetened yogurt. The two bacteria operate at significantly different rates, with *Lactobacillus* petering out in just the first few weeks, while the pedio can continue as long as two years to complete its cycle. Therefore, beers that are younger than a year old and contain pedio will continue to increase in sourness. Lambic beers are typically blended with young (not wholly fermented) beer immediately prior to bottling for conditioning and will continue to grow in sourness in the first year or so in the cellar.

The naturally occurring lacto and pedio in a lambic tend to stop producing as the beer becomes either too acidic (below pH 3.4) or too high in alcohol (above 8 percent). Because of this, lambics often hover around the 5 percent ABV mark to ensure a comfortable environment for the bacteria to work.

While the lacto and pedio bacteria are doing their work, the yeast *Brettanomyces* ("brett") is busy too. As brett ferments, it creates distinctive alcohols and organic acids that combine to create a variety of unique aromatic esters and phenols. Brett also makes some lactic and acetic acids, but the amount of these sour-tasting acids produced is minimal compared with the amounts created from the lacto and pedio. Blended lambic beers (gueuzes, for example) always include some amount of young, one-year-old lambic to ensure that there will be sufficient, viable pedio and brett left to bottle-condition the beer.

Because of its long fermentation and conditioning phases, brett will continue to scavenge oxygen for a much longer period than *Saccharomyces*. Beers containing brett, therefore, are often relatively free of oxidative effects. This is crucial information in thinking about the development of a beer with brett: The normal oxidation flavors of toffee, sherry, and others will not be present, or, if they are, only to a small degree. Also, the fresh ester and hop profiles will stay vibrant longer due to these antioxidant properties of the brett. Additionally, brett consumes many off-flavors associated with *Saccharomyces* autolysis.

In time (typically around a year), the traditional brett-produced phenols and acids will develop to a level detectable to most tasters. The flavors from these unique compounds are described as "funky" or "barnyardy" and bring to mind wet leather, horse sweat, and washed-rind cheese. The primary phenols responsible for these flavors are 4-ethylphenol (4-EP) and

Breweries are beginning to use cultured
Brettanomyces as their yeast of choice.

4-ethylguaiacol (4-EG) and are a result of brett's synthesis of traditional fermentation phenols like 4-vinylguaiacol and 4-vinylphenol (pepper, clove). The amount of 4-EP and 4-EG produced is finite and dependent on the amount of initial fermentation phenols present. Therefore, the amount of "funkiness" in a lambic beer does not often increase with age since the majority of 4-EP and 4-EG has been produced and is already present. A very small increase may be observed in gueuze in the first few years due to the one-year-old portion of the blend, though after that the flavor slowly degrades.

In addition to the traditional lambic beers, many other beers are brewed with the same microbiota, although not necessarily all in tandem. The United States has witnessed a growing trend of brewers fermenting beers using *Brettanomyces* instead of *Saccharomyces,* most notably Anchorage Brewing Company and Crooked Stave.

Just as with *Sacchromyces,* there is a wide variety of brett strains, and many of the new, lab-cultured strains are capable of developing strong fruity esters with a minimum of the traditional "funky" phenols and acids. These esters are often reminiscent of pineapple, apricot, and fresh flowers, giving the beers an intense bouquet. Brett is a particularly aggressive yeast, however, eating any and all available sugars and leaving a very dry beer. With the esters faded and little residual sugar to provide the malt flavors a base to stand on, any brett-derived phenols can become one-dimensional and quite unpleasant after a few years. Consequently, many "funky" brett beers are best drunk in the first year or two of cellaring, when the various components are developed but still balanced. It appears that the "cleaner," less phenolic lab-cultured brett beers can be cellared a great deal longer.

Other beers, rather than being fermented exclusively with brett, simply receive a small addition prior to bottling. This approach aids in the consumption of residual oxygen and enables the development of brett-associated complexities during aging. One noteworthy example is the classic Trappist brew Orval. Dry-hopped before being spiked with brett, it's pleasantly hoppy and honey-tinged when drunk fresh. Given a year in the bottle, however, their unique brett strain transforms the beer into a crisp, floral ale with layers of brett-induced intricacy. It continues to develop over the years, but most find it overwhelmingly phenolic around the three-year mark.

Das Berliner Weiße

The German wheat beer style known as Berliner Weiße is brewed with *Lactobacillus*, which gives the beer its characteristically dry, tart flavor. The lactic-acid creation occurs in the brewery, and so these beers typically do not become more sour in the cellar. However, there is usually some brett integrated in the fermentation process, allowing the style to develop in the cellar — though the bready, wheat flavor will disappear after the first few months.

Acetobacter, the last of the microbiota to touch on here, is never used singularly in beer. The bacteria in this group are often freeloaders, lurking in barrels and producing acetic acid (vinegar) — a very undesirable component in most beers, even lambics. They feed off oxygen and will turn any beer into malt vinegar given enough oxygen and time.

One of the few places where *Acetobacter* are somewhat welcome is Flanders red and brown ales, styles to which they offer a characteristically mild sour flavor. The acetic sourness they create comes from the time they spend in the porous, oxygen-rich oak barrels in which they're traditionally aged. Once bottled, they're usually pasteurized or filtered. Now lacking much of the oxygen-scavenging brett yeast, these beers develop sweet oxidation-derived flavors in the cellar, and when these flavors pair with the sourness, the result is a rich, decadent beer.

CHAPTER 3

The Best Beer Styles for Your Cellar

Time for the fun part: tasting! Whether you're savoring a vintage beer or tasting a fresh beer to determine its cellaring potential, your approach should be different from when you're downing your average brew. One of the main reasons for aging beer is to allow new, sometimes subtle flavors to develop and emerge and thus add layers of complexity. So be sure not to rush the tasting and miss out on the little aspects that make vintage beer so special.

To help boost your knowledge and guide you along in the tasting process, it's a good idea to follow the standard beer-tasting procedure. Evaluate the aroma of your aged beer first, and then carefully examine the appearance of the beer. Has the clarity or color changed over time? When taking that first sip, swirl it around in your mouth to ensure all the different taste receptors get utilized. And don't forget to pay attention to the mouthfeel of the beer. Has the body gotten thinner or fuller? Did the carbonation hold up? Have the alcohol aspects softened?

Formal Tasting Procedure

Though there may be a few tasters who can easily focus their attention on the various aspects of a beer they're evaluating, most of us benefit from following the standard tasting procedure. Following a Beer Scoresheet from the Beer Judge Certification Program (BJCP) can help to jog your senses. Being obliged to write down your perceptions is one of the best ways to sharpen your tasting skills. A sample Scoresheet is included in References, and copies can be downloaded at www.bjcp.org.

Many of the flavors encountered in aged beer are different from those in fresh beers. Use the Vintage Beer Tasting Wheel (opposite) to help you identify some of the more common flavor characteristics unique to cellared beer.

Equipped with the knowledge of how different aspects of beer change over time, you're in a good position to judge which beer styles will show improvement when cellared. There are 82 beer styles recognized by the Beer Judge Certification Program, and of those, in my view only the following six styles will regularly show improvement with aging:

1. **English barley wines (and old ales)**

2. **American barley wines**

3. **Imperial stouts**

4. **Belgian quads**

5. **Flanders red and brown ales**

6. **Gueuzes**

That's not to say that *all* beers of these styles will improve with age, nor that beers of styles not on this list won't, but this is the safe-bet list. A few styles that could arguably be on it are Baltic porters, rauchbiers, tripels, and dubbels; all these styles have examples that age exceptionally well. But, because these styles also have plenty of examples that are much better fresh than aged, they need to be judged on a case-by-case basis.

VINTAGE BEER TASTING WHEEL

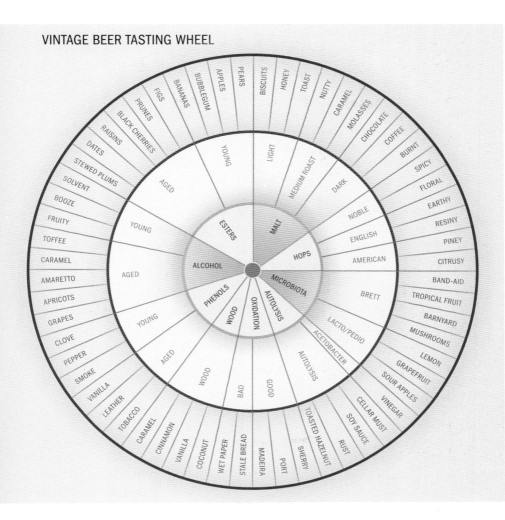

ENGLISH BARLEY WINES

The granddaddy of all vintage beers, English barley wines undeniably return the richest results when cellared. Most of this comes from the fact that these beers are built to age, as opposed to beers built to be drunk young but that also happen to improve with age. The English brewers who first created these beers envisioned them being laid down for years to mellow and develop.

The English barley wine
is the noblest of vintage
beers.

English barley wines are a showcase of everything the English love in their beers: malty richness, fruity yeast esters, and a complementary hop bitterness. The malt component is key to why these ales age so well. By utilizing extremely long boil times, intense, complex melanoidins are created via kettle caramelization, enabling the beer to develop sherry and Madeira-like flavors over time that add a delicious intricacy. In addition, the traditional yeast strains used have low attenuation, which when paired with an overwhelming amount of malt sugars, leaves behind a good quantity of residual sugars. These sugars help sustain the body of the beer as the proteins fall out and slow the oxidation process via reductones when combined with the melanoidins.

The yeast is another vital part as to why these ales age so well. The English ale yeasts tend to throw off considerable fruity esters and fusel alcohols when strained by such a high volume of fermentable sugars. As the esters and fusel alcohols develop and oxidize, they take on prominent candied fruit flavors and aromas, often reminiscent of fruitcake. With the very high alcohol levels present in these beers (9–12 percent), the development is slow enough to allow the deep, rich flavors to emerge.

A major difference between English and American barley wines is the hop component. Though less hoppy than their American counterparts, the English barley wines can still be fairly bitter. However, the hops typically used are of the English varieties and are quite high in beta acids relative to alpha acids. This favorable ratio allows the bitterness to fade at a slower rate and with a reduced potential of cardboard flavors because of fewer isomerized alpha acids.

English barley wine's little brother, old ale, should be considered as well, although they'll exhibit a faster aging process at their reduced ABV.

AGING EXPECTATIONS

A decent English barley wine will easily continue to develop positive characteristics for 6 to 8 years, with some examples capable of 10 to 15 years. Exceptional versions have been known to go 50-plus years in the proper conditions, but very few beers are currently being brewed with the residual sugar and fusel levels needed to justify this amount of aging. Stronger old ales (around 8 percent ABV) can typically be expected to improve for 3 to 4 years.

Classic English Barley Wine Candidates

- AleSmith Old Numbskull

- Avery Samael's Ale

- Eldridge Pope Thomas Hardy's Ale (no longer brewed, but bottles can still be found)

- Fuller's Vintage Ale (old ale)

- Hair of the Dog Adam (old world ale)

- J.W. Lees Harvest Ale

- Midnight Sun Arctic Devil

- North Coast Old Stock Ale (old ale)

- Weyerbacher Blithering Idiot

AMERICAN BARLEY WINES

American barley wines are known to be drier, cleaner versions of their English brethren. Typically made with the mind-set that they should be drunk immediately, they're brewed with heaping amounts of American hops and tend also to be less sweet and malty. In general, most will fall somewhere between an English barley wine and a double IPA.

Some people would say you shouldn't waste time aging American barley wines. They argue that they aren't malty enough, their IBU levels are too high, and their yeast isn't fruity enough. While all this may be true, they have one thing going for them that English barley wines do not: massive availability and a great price. American barley wines are available from practically every American brewery, and you can still find them in the cellar-friendly 12-ounce, six-pack format. Plus, they cost half (or even less) what you pay for a J.W. Lees Harvest Ale or a similar English barley wine.

Carefully chosen American barley wines showcase a full balance of aged flavors and hoppiness.

All right, so pricing and availability are obvious positives, but there is nothing worse than patiently waiting for a beer to come of age only to crack it and find a stale, dull mess. Therefore, when looking for American barley wines to cellar, it's of utmost importance to analyze the beer's makeup. Foremost, you need to critically evaluate its hop content. The lower the IBU the better, since an abundance of hops is what often contributes to the oxidization-derived cardboard flavors. Also, some American hop varieties, such as Cascade, which is higher in hop beta acids, age better than others.

The vast majority of American barley wines will improve if cellared for six months to a year.

Next, be sure to look for a full, rich malt presence. Ask yourself how the balance will be affected once those hops have faded. Be aware that many brewers, in an attempt to showcase their hop profile, will tone back the malts and residual sugars, which will leave a thin, unpleasant beer after cellaring.

Recommendations are another great source of help in choosing the right American barley wines. Given how prominent hops are in these beers, it's often hard to guess how they will develop, so don't hesitate to make use of trusted opinions to guide you. Sometimes reviews at websites such as beeradvocate.com can give you a good idea of aging potential if you take the time to comb through them and find reviews of vintage bottles. Use caution, though, since many online reviewers are far from being experts.

AGING EXPECTATIONS

The vast majority of American barley wines will improve if cellared for 6 months to a year. In an effort to free up brewing space, breweries often rush these beers to market, so this minimal aging period will allow the alcohol to mellow slightly and the hops to integrate better into the overall profile. Beers that have proven themselves age-worthy display a broad range of optimal cellaring times because of their varying hop profiles and malt bills. The average length is 2 to 3 years, with the most exceptional examples improving for up to 10 years (very rare).

Classic American Barley Wine Candidates

- Alaskan Barley Wine Ale

- Bell's Third Coast Old Ale

- Dogfish Head Olde School Barleywine

- Hair of the Dog Doggie Claws

- Lagunitas Olde GnarlyWine

- Rogue Old Crustacean Barley Wine

- Sierra Nevada Bigfoot

- Smuttynose Barleywine Style Ale

IMPERIAL STOUTS

A style popular in Catherine the Great's Russian court, this stout had to be brewed to alcohol, residual sugar, and hopping levels that would ensure the beer would survive the long journey from England. Though its popularity decreased over the years, the modern brewer's penchant for high-hopped, high-gravity ales has led to a massive resurgence of the style.

Essentially a dark, roasted version of a barley wine, imperial stouts show a vast array of both roasted character and hop levels. Analyzing the malt-bill makeup of these beers is crucial to determining how well they will age. Many brewers use large quantities of highly roasted malts to give an intense, coffeelike flavor. As they age, this initial acrid character softens into a dark-chocolate flavor that is quite enjoyable. If the beer has fruity esters or was made using beta-rich hops, the chocolate flavor can combine to create black cherry or even berry aspects. However, due to the highly roasted malts, imperial stouts will show sherry and caramel flavors sooner and in a higher intensity than, say, a barley wine. This faster development shortens their cellaring time.

Something else to be aware of with these beers is the effects of autolysis, or yeast degradation, which can give rise to off flavors often described as "meaty." While any beer bottled with live yeast is susceptible to autolysis,

Imperial stouts often take on dark-chocolate and stone-fruit flavors after aging.

in a beer that also features a highly roasted malt character, the associated off flavors are particularly unpleasant, reminiscent of ink, soy sauce, or even blood. It is theorized too that stouts are more susceptible to autolysis because of the highly acidic nature of the roasted malts, which accelerates yeast degradation.

Using an alkaline water helps to offset the acidity and so keep those unwanted flavors in check longer. This is most likely the reason that the classic Courage Russian Imperial Stout, brewed with the alkaline-rich waters of London, has been known to age for multiple decades. In addition, these beers were aged longer before bottling, which allowed the yeast to better settle out, ultimately resulting in fewer yeast cells in the bottle. Unfortunately, many of the classic English breweries that first brewed this style no longer produce these stouts. Modern brewers interested in creating age-worthy strong stouts would do well to appropriately treat their water and pay close attention to bottled-yeast content.

> **Worthy examples will improve for two to three years before beginning to develop off-tastes from the autolysis.**

As with barley wines, hop amount and type, as well as residual sugar levels, are crucial to the cellar potential of a beer of this style. Watch out for highly hopped versions, which could produce wet-cardboard flavors. Also keep an eye out for examples with low residual sugars; they'll thin over time, creating dull beers.

AGING EXPECTATIONS

Depending on hop and roasted-malt levels, this style exhibits a wide range of aging time frames. However, almost all will benefit from a year of aging, unless the drinker is looking to maintain high-roast or high-hop flavors. Worthy examples will improve for two to three years before beginning to succumb to negative oxidized flavors and off-tastes from the autolysis. Exceptional examples can endure and improve for decades, but these are admittedly very rare.

Classic Imperial Stout Candidates

- Bell's Expedition Stout

- Brooklyn Brewery Black Chocolate Stout

- Courage Russian Imperial Stout (not brewed since 1993, but vintage bottles still drinking well. Re-released by Wells and Young in 2011, long-term aging potential unknown, but shows promise)

- Deschutes The Abyss

- Founders Imperial Stout

- Goose Island Bourbon County Brand Stout

- Midnight Sun Berserker Imperial Stout

- Stone Imperial Russian Stout

- Three Floyds Dark Lord Imperial Stout

BELGIAN QUADS

Officially referred to as a Belgian dark strong ale, Belgian quads obtained their moniker from the country's monastic tradition of naming beers in terms of alcohol strength. Quadrupel, quad for short, is the obvious next step after the Belgian enkel (Flemish for "single"; an almost extinct style), dubbel, and tripel. The term was adopted into the beer world by the Dutch Trappist brewery La Trappe, which calls its strongest offering (10 percent ABV) Quadrupel.

A Belgian quad can conveniently be thought of as a Belgian barley wine. They're similar in color and alcohol content to American and English barley wines, but they're typically drier, yeastier, and essentially without hop character. The yeast profile has notes of cherry, fig, and plum, similar to a barley wine, though at much higher levels. Additionally, this style typically contains spicy, pepperlike phenols that take the place of hops to help cut through the maltiness. As quads age, the fruity esters develop into dried-fruit flavors, and the phenols take on vanilla and tobacco or leather notes. While these transformed phenols are often pleasant, they also bring the risk

Belgian quads, essentially Belgian barley wines, can benefit from aging, just as their American and English counterparts.

that the beer will be unbalanced once they're gone, similar to the situation with hops.

Another reason these beers age well is their high level of fusel alcohols. Given their fusel-apt Belgian yeast strains, high fermentable sugars, and warmer-than-average fermentation temperature, they're usually ripe with higher alcohols. A few years in the cellar will oxidize these alcohols into aldehydes that can lend the beer toffee, caramel, and even chocolate flavors.

> **As quads age, the fruity esters develop into dried-fruit flavors.**

The minimal amount of hops used are there only to provide a subtle bittering component to cut the maltiness. Common hop varieties are Styrian Golding, noble, or English types, all of which have a favorable beta-acid ratio, allowing the beer to age well without generating degraded hop flavors.

While the quad's lighter version, the dubbel, has been known to age well, quads have the alcohol content to go the distance in the cellar and are the better choice considering the relatively high cost of either of these Trappist brews.

AGING EXPECTATIONS

Aging Belgian quads, already quite complex and delicious fresh, helps to mellow the alcohol and yeast aspects and develop new flavors that continue to add to their complexity. Exceptional examples have been known to drink well for up to 30 years, but 5 years is generally optimal. This is plenty of time for the esters to take on dried-fruit notes and for the sweet aldehydes to appear but isn't so long as to thin out these already dry ales.

Classic Belgian Quad Candidates

- **Chimay Grande Réserve**
- **De Struise Pannepot (all variations)**
- **Gouden Carolus Grand Cru of the Emperor**
- **La Trappe Quadrupel**

- Lost Abbey Judgment Day
- Ommegang Three Philosophers (A quad spiked with *kriek* [cherry lambic], this beer becomes overwhelmed with brett phenols after about three years but develops beautifully up to that point.)
- Russian River Salvation
- Trappistes Rochefort 10
- Westvleteren 12

FLANDERS RED AND BROWN ALES

Often referred to as the Burgundy of Belgium, the Flanders red, with its strong cherry/strawberry esters and acidic, tannic bitterness, is reminiscent of red wine. In fact, with its ruby hue (from kettle caramelization of the malt during very prolonged boils and oxidation in the wood), this beer could be mistaken for a glass of wine if not for the slight white head.

This ale is traditionally aged for at least a year in large oak vats (called *foeders*) similar to those used in the port industry. These casks are responsible for much of the uniqueness in flavor of Flanders red and are typically used by the breweries for decades, if not centuries, as is the case at the famed Rodenbach brewery. The actual oak character in these beers is minimal, however, since the vats are used so many times. The oak's primary function is to serve as a home for the resident bacteria and yeast necessary to create the winelike acidic character typical of this style.

The types of microbiota in the foeders vary from brewery to brewery but generally comprise a mix of *Lactobacillus*, *Pediococcus*, and *Brettanomyces*. In most cases, these beers are pasteurized prior to bottling in an effort to maintain some sweetness in the beer. While they are certainly a sour beer, the funky brett complexities found in lambics are masked by the combination of relatively high residual sugars and lactic and acetic acids. The beer is traditionally blended prior to bottling, much like wine. Well-aged sour beer is cut with less-acidic, younger beer to balance the sour and sweet characters.

Over time, the winelike Flanders red ale often develops
sweet, oxidized flavors, creating an enjoyable complexity.

Though most examples have some degree of acetic (vinegar) character from the vats' resident *Acetobacter*, it is not particularly desirable and a noticeable amount is considered a fault. So avoid aging beers with a detectable vinegar flavor, since they'll take on nail polish flavors over time. It's the acidic nature of this style, which acts as a preservative, that enables it to age gracefully despite its relatively low ABV (about 6 percent).

The Flanders brown ale (*oud bruin*) is a less-sour, maltier version of a Flanders red, and this style also ages exceptionally well. The only reason it doesn't have a dedicated write-up here is because there are few commercial examples available. Expect the brown to age similarly to a Flanders red but with more aged malt flavors. Good examples are De Dolle Oerbier Special Reserva, Deschutes The Dissident, and Liefmans Goudenband.

AGING EXPECTATIONS

Versions that include a portion of young beer in their blend will lessen in malty sweetness in the first few years. Subsequent aging shows an increase in the sour acidity and oak flavors that are no longer masked by the residual sugars. Over time the beers will develop oxidization-based malt flavors like toffee and caramel, adding to their complexity. Most will improve for at least 2 to 3 years, but exceptional examples can go for 20 or more.

Classic Flanders Ale Candidates

- The Bruery Oude Tart
- Crooked Stave Origins
- The Lost Abbey Red Poppy Ale
- New Belgium La Folie
- Ommegang Rouge
- Panil Barriquée Sour
- Rodenbach Grand Cru

Beer Decanting

Sometimes vintage beers, especially those with *Brettanomyces* and/ or phenols, give off a somewhat unpleasant mustiness when first opened. On these occasions, decanting the beer (just as you would a wine) often allows these disagreeable flavors to blow off. In most cases 10 to 30 minutes should do the trick.

GUEUZES

One of the most intricate, graceful beer styles, gueuze has the distinction of being required to be aged. The result of an artful blending of one-, two-, and three-year-old lambics, it achieves a wealth of unique flavors that can be attained only by open fermentation, turbid mashing, aged hops, and time. The wort is cooled in large, open copper pans to collect the ambient micro-biota, and then it's fermented in oak casks.

During the first year of aging, a strong, lactic-acid flavor develops as the *Brettanomyces*, *Pediococcus*, and *Lactobacillus* team up and go to work. Further aging brings out funky, barnyard aspects like horse sweat and hay as well as fruity grapefruit and pineapple flavors. There is often also the slightest taste of oak. During the second and third years of aging, the *Brettanomyces* slowly consume the residual sugars, drying out the beer in the process.

A skilled gueuze blender will mix some of all three vintages to create a beer that balances the sweet-sourness of the young lambic and the funky dry-ness of the old. The finished product should not exhibit the one-dimensional sweet and sour of a young unblended lambic but, rather, a melding of this character with oak, barnyard funk, and fruitiness.

Thanks to the antioxidant nature of brett and gueuze's acidic makeup, it stands up remarkably well to the oxidation so typical of many aged beers. Because of this, the caramel and sherry notes found in most vintage beers never form to much of a degree. These aspects are also why, even with a relatively low ABV (4–6 percent), gueuzes can age for so long.

The strong sour and funky notes in gueuze and its lambic counterparts soften with time, allowing subtle flavors such as pineapple and hazelnut to shine.

There is a common misconception that aging a gueuze will make it more acidic. Although there is an increase in sourness during the first few years (as the *Brettanomyces* and pedio consume the young portion of the blend, creating more acidity), the sourness typically softens with time, lessening tartness. As the brett slowly synthesizes the acids into esters, a range of the flavors can appear that were previously overshadowed: must, rhubarb, and honey, to name a few. As gueuzes become very old (seven or more years), they may seem to taste more sour because all the other flavors have faded to a much greater degree than the sourness, even though no additional acidity has been created.

Though the fruit character fades somewhat, vintage fruit lambics can still be delicious in their own right.

In addition to gueuze, there are a number of fruit-steeped lambics made by these same producers. These beers are often a blended lambic with fruit added to the cask partway through aging. As with a gueuze, you'll see the *Brettanomyces* slowly ferment all the sugars, including the additional fruit sugars. With time, this increases the lambic character and reduces the fruit aspects. This is not necessarily bad, since the fruit character in a young lambic can sometimes be overwhelming. Very often a fruit lambic improves if aged for a year or two. Aging beyond that is a tricky balancing act. Cherries maintain their fruit flavor quite well, while raspberries fade quickly and become astringent. Be that as it may, one of the best beers I've ever drunk was a 25-year-old raspberry lambic that, because of the fruit, displayed a dazzling array of distinctive flavors that could never be found in even the finest aged gueuze.

AGING EXPECTATIONS

Already considerably aged by the time it's available for purchase and carefully blended to create a balanced, ready-to-drink beer, a gueuze is quite enjoyable "fresh." However, as seen in the flavor profile charts on the next page, a young gueuze is sometimes "spiky," declaring a variety of very prominent flavor aspects. In time these spikes are worn down, and a more compact flavor profile evolves, which allows some of the more subtle flavors to come forward — an excellent justification for cellaring these already superb beers.

Classic Gueuze Candidates

- Boon Oude Geuze
- Cantillon Gueuze
- De Cam Oude Geuze
- Drie Fonteinen Oude Geuze
- Girardin Gueuze (Black Label)
- Hanssens Oude Gueuze
- Lindemans Gueuze Cuvée René

PERCEIVED FLAVORS OF FRESH GUEUZE

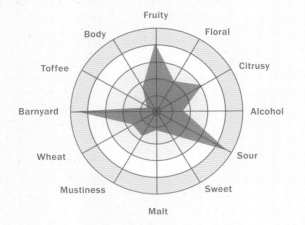

PERCEIVED FLAVORS OF 10-YEAR GUEUZE

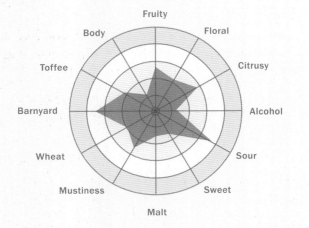

Comparison of the perceived flavors of aged gueuze.

Food and Vintage Beer Pairings

As beer gains acceptance in the culinary world, people are growing more comfortable with the idea of skipping the wine and instead pairing beer with their favorite dishes at home and in restaurants. Vintage beer brings a host of new flavors to the table that can create a bevy of exciting food-and-beer combinations. When pairing a high ABV beer, look to match it up with an item of equal flavor intensity. The strong alcohol presence of a barley wine would decimate the delicate nature of white fish, but would complement a steak just like a cabernet. When it comes to sour beers, look for something sweet or creamy to contrast with the acidity and still allow the beer's nuances to shine. Here are a few of my favorite combinations:

ENGLISH BARLEY WINE AND STILTON CHEESE: The sharp, salty creaminess of Great Britain's finest blue cheese is the perfect contrast to the rich dried fruit and toffee notes of this beer.

AMERICAN BARLEY WINE AND CRÈME BRULEE: The bitterness of the American barley wine is a counterpoint to the dessert's intense caramelized sugars.

GUEUZE AND SHEEP'S MILK CHEESE: For one of the most complex beer styles available, a simple creamy cheese is all that is needed to give this acidic beer a platform from which to shine.

IMPERIAL STOUT AND RASPBERRY MOUSSE: The raspberry helps to draw out the complementary dark fruit notes of the beer, while its creaminess contrasts with the roasted malts.

FLANDER'S RED ALE AND PHEASANT: Similar to a French Burgundy, this beer uses acidity to cut through the richness of the game: a new twist on an old classic.

BELGIAN QUAD AND CARBONADE FLAMANDE: The relative dryness of the beer makes a great match to the heartiness of this sweet Belgian beef stew.

CHAPTER 4

Tasting Classic Cellar Beers

Now that you've worked your way through what makes vintage beers great, it's time to get to the really interesting part: real-world aging results! To give a leg up to anyone new on the cellaring scene, I include here write-ups for classic, yet common, age-worthy beers. With just a glance you can see the results of years of my beer hunting and tasting.

Each of the classic cellaring styles discussed in chapter 3 has a representative here; and all of them feature, in my view, a good combination of potential and availability. Westvleteren 12, for example, is an exceptionally impressive cellaring candidate for Belgian quads, but if you have to go to the monastery to get it, there's no point in discussing it. In addition to the six classics, there are a few other notable beers that have proven to return exceptional results.

Each write-up contains an evaluation of a fresh version of the beer, as well as how it ages. To obtain this information, a panel of experienced vintage beer aficionados conducted tastings of multiple vintages of the beer (called a vertical tasting).

To ensure as objective an assessment as possible, the following conditions were imposed:

1. **Whenever possible, all beers were cellared under the same conditions. Cellar temperature was kept between 55 and 65°F (13–18°C).**

2. **The tasters on the panel were the same for each beer and style.**

3. **Each beer was served at the same temperature and in the same shape glass.**

A vertical of East End's Gratitude waits to be opened.

Tastings were of vintages up to 10 years of age, though older bottles were sampled in a few styles. However, beers older than 15 years were not included because of the extended effects of bottle-to-bottle variation.

The tasting results were condensed into an aging profile chart to graphically represent the changes that occur as a beer ages. The aspects tracked for each beer varied according to what was crucial to the particular style.

While tasting is admittedly subjective, these appraisals should give you an idea of how certain beers (and to some degree certain styles) are likely to progress over time.

J.W. LEES HARVEST ALE

STYLE: English barley wine

ABV: 11.4%

BOTTLE SIZE: 9.4 fl. oz.

HISTORY: Though J.W. Lees Brewery of Middleton, England, has been crafting quality beer since 1876, it wasn't until 1986 that it released this delectable sipper into the world. Brewed with the choicest Maris Otter malt and East Kent Golding hops, it has the legs to go the distance. The brewery uses a house-developed yeast strain to ferment the brew in original open copper-lined vessels.

Showing balanced sweetness along with dried fruit and tobacco complexities, this barley wine peaks at 13 years old.

Given the fickleness of the season's crop, a slight year-to-year variation can be detected, much like with wine. Prior to bottling, the beer is aged for two months, although it tends to show up across the pond two years later (at the earliest).

FRESH TASTING CRITIQUE

NOTE: *Considering brewery aging, transportation time, and distributor storage, the freshest this beer can usually be tasted in the United States is two years old.*

APPEARANCE: Hazy, copper colored, with a small amount of brown sediment; low, creamy, white head.

SMELL: Bread pudding, burnt sugar, and honey mingle with fruity esters reminiscent of dried apricot. Earthy hop aroma; fair initial alcohol presence.

TASTE: The malts come forward with a nutty, honey-tinged flavor, but there is a presence of chalk and iodine lurking in the background. The hops are relatively subdued but still present. Alcohol presence is warming and slightly fruity. Slight cardboard flavor.

MOUTHFEEL: Very thick and chewy. Carbonation cuts through the fullness well.

OVERALL IMPRESSION: This drinks well right off the bat, with the alcohol being fairly well integrated (though it does already have two years on it) and a pleasant balance between the malt and hops. The hint of iodine adds complexity.

AGING EXPECTATIONS

Tasting this beer fresh brought up no obvious aspects that demand further aging. However, the fruity fusels, English hops, and deep malt flavors beckon the cellarer. As it ages, this beer can integrate its flavors even more and add a host of new ones.

APPEARANCE: Over the span of about ten years, the malt proteins slowly oxidize and the hazy copper color develops into a deep garnet hue. Carbonation is variable from year to year. In general, it slowly declines; it was nonexistent at the 13-year mark, and bottles as young as four years old had no carbonation.

SMELL: The first few vintages showed a quick mellowing of the alcohol presence. Concurrently, even sweeter toffee and caramel flavors come forward and continue to mount until almost the ten-year mark. Hop aroma becomes imperceptible after about four years. As the hops fade, notes of dried fruit appear, predominantly raisin. By year five, a definitive sherry aroma is present and becomes the dominant feature. Bottles past ten years have a slight umami flavor and hints of tobacco and blackberry jam.

TASTE: The initial sweet flavors continue to grow over the first few vintages. The seaside iodine flavors don't last long and couldn't be detected after five years of aging. The hop bitterness fades linearly, leaving the beer overwhelmingly sweet around five to six years old. At this point sherry and dried fruit flavors arise, providing some complexity in what would otherwise be a cloying brew.

As the malts continue to age, flavors of molasses and burnt sugar begin to appear. The dried-fruit esters become more pronounced but still struggle to rise above the dominating sweet flavors.

After year ten the beer really settles into its own, with the sweetness at a level that allows the other flavors to make themselves known. At this point hints of tobacco, leather, and soy sauce appear.

MOUTHFEEL: The mouthfeel grows over the first three or so years of aging and then slowly degrades. First-year bottles were thin. However, even after a decade of cellaring, the beer is still impressively full-bodied. It should be noted that the trend of decreasing carbonation can greatly increase the perceived malt body.

OVERALL IMPRESSION: This is an incredibly rewarding beer to cellar. It undergoes a range of developments and shows substantial changes year to year, especially beyond the five-year mark. Our tasting panel agreed that the vintages of 12 or 13 years were optimal since they weren't overwhelmingly sweet (relative to the style) and had developed a variety of complex flavors that made the sipping an enjoyably contemplative experience. Older bottles (not included in the chart) were found to be too thin and the flavors too muted.

Fans of aromatic, sweet, sherrylike barley wines would probably best enjoy those in the range of eight to ten years, while Scotch fans will appreciate the seaside aspects of bottles less than five years old.

J.W. LEES HARVEST ALE AGING PROFILE

INTENSITY

MOUTHFEEL

SWEET AROMA/TASTE
SHERRY

DRIED FRUIT/WINE
BITTERNESS

0   14

YEARS AGED

SIERRA NEVADA BIGFOOT

STYLE: American barley wine

ABV: 9.6%

BOTTLE SIZE: 12 fl. oz.

HISTORY: In 1980, Sierra Nevada's flagship brew, Sierra Nevada Pale Ale, was born, a distinctly "West Coast" interpretation of the classic British pale ale that met with quick success thanks to its delightfully hoppy yet complex profile. Bigfoot emerged three years later when the brewery decided to apply this same West Coast approach to the English barley wine style. What many consider to be the quintessential American barley wine, Bigfoot pairs an intense amount of hops with a significant malty richness and high ABV.

Displaying emerging sherry flavors and a retained hoppiness, this American barley wine is best at five years old.

With this combo, founders Ken Grossman and Paul Camusi didn't intend for Bigfoot to be aged, but enjoyed fresh to capture its extreme hop character. It wasn't long, though, until curious beer cellarers began stashing away a bottle or two from their six-packs. And what was discovered is that this beer undergoes a remarkable transformation. With Sierra Nevada's vast distribution and low price point (currently about $2 a bottle), it quickly became a cellar staple. Because of the brewery's careful attention to oxygen pickup, a very long boil, copious amounts of the beta-rich Cascade hop, and bottle-conditioning, this beer is able to beat the odds and avoid the cardboard pitfalls of many American barley wines.

FRESH TASTING CRITIQUE

APPEARANCE: Pours with a hefty, long-lasting, off-white head that leaves a clinging lace on the glass. Brilliantly clear amber color with a garnet hue.

SMELL: A wallop of hoppiness with loads of pine sap and grapefruit.

As the beer breathes, caramel malt comes forward, followed by very light stone-fruit esters. Low, fruity alcohol presence, but not to a fault.

TASTE: Incredibly bitter and hoppy. The resin/citrus hop flavors are powerful and pound the taste buds. There is a deep, nutty, caramel maltiness that throws a counterpunch to the hops. Fruity esters and fusel alcohol are detectable, though faint, in the background, with notes of apricot and date.

MOUTHFEEL: The hop bitterness is contrasted by the creaminess of the alcohol and fullness of the malt bill. With its medium-high carbonation, the beer is balanced, yet intense.

OVERALL IMPRESSION: Though Bigfoot is a hop heavyweight, it's also thick and malty with a touch of fruitiness. Those looking for more malt and ester complexity than in a double IPA should thoroughly enjoy this quintessential American barley wine.

AGING EXPECTATIONS

With its telltale malty richness and high ABV, Bigfoot can reasonably be expected to stand up in the cellar for a good amount of time, even with its high hop content. The main concern is whether the hops will oxidize into those ruinous stale flavors that many American barley wines can acquire. Happily, experience has shown that those aspects are kept to a minimum, and the developing sherry flavors, along with an impressively stoic hop presence, make this a worthwhile cellaring candidate for those who still want a hop presence in their aged beer.

APPEARANCE: In time, the amber color darkens as oxidation sets in. There was a substantial increase in hue starting with the 2007 vintage, which, not coincidentally, was the last year the cap was a twist-off.

Carbonation decreased, but even the ten-year-old bottle released a fair, albeit low, hiss. The twist-off vintages saw an appreciable reduction in carbonation.

SMELL: The overwhelming hop bouquet of a fresh bottle remains a prominent player through the years. It fades impressively slowly and is still more powerful than any malt presence until about three years old (though by year six the hop aroma is nearly gone). This is not to say that notes of caramel malts aren't present — just that the hops are in the forefront. As the malts begin to oxidize, strong sherry notes arise around the third year and gradually increase until leveling off after about seven years. Sweet toffee flavors appear in tandem with the sherry feature, but never to much of a degree. Dried-fruit flavors are also present (year four or so) but fail to become much of a component in the aged beer.

TASTE: Just as in the aroma, the main player here is the hops. However, unlike the hoppy aroma's eventual fade, the flavor of even our ten-year-old bottle had a decent amount of hop bitterness and a few touches of resiny hops. Sherry flavors from the oxidizing kettle-caramelized melanoidins appear around the third year and steadily increase throughout the years. While a cardboard flavor comes with the sherry, it remains a minimal part of the beer and is easily overlooked. Additionally, this flavor doesn't seem to increase over time but quickly levels off.

Notably, the dried-fruit and toffee flavors so omnipresent in many aged

SIERRA NEVADA BIGFOOT (CONTINUED)

English barley wines never amount to much in this beer. This is most likely due to the relatively low level of fruity esters and fusels in the beer initially. Considering its high ABV, it drinks impressively clean when young; although an enjoyable aspect at the time, this handicaps the potential of the vintage bottles. Still, since the brewers never intended for this beer to be aged, it's no big surprise.

MOUTHFEEL: So impressively thick and malty as a fresh beer, it maintains a full body over the years. The slight alcohol presence ages gracefully, though bottles just a few years old taste boozier due to the fading hops, which initially hid much of this quality.

OVERALL IMPRESSION: Bigfoot (as with most American barley wines) never quite achieves some of the complexities of its English brethren. Flavors and aromas like leather, port, hazelnut, and fig never make much of an appearance. However, it does something that the English barley wines never pull off, and that is to combine quality, aged malt flavors (sherry) and an extraordinary hop presence. Along with its relatively minimal cardboard flavor, this combination is fantastic and makes a strong case for a spot in anyone's cellar. The panel deemed the bottles of four to five years old as optimal since they still have a notable hop aura, a robust sherry flavor, and mellowed alcohol bite. That doesn't mean that older bottles aren't good — quite to the contrary. Rather, they lack the complexity that justifies sitting on a beer for eight to ten years.

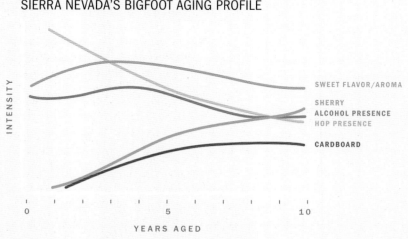

SIERRA NEVADA'S BIGFOOT AGING PROFILE

INTENSITY

SWEET FLAVOR/AROMA
SHERRY
ALCOHOL PRESENCE
HOP PRESENCE

CARDBOARD

0   5   10

YEARS AGED

DRIE FONTEINEN OUDE GEUZE

STYLE: Oude geuze

ABV: 6%

BOTTLE SIZE: 375 mL

HISTORY: Having mastered the craft of blending lambic from his father, Armand Debelder has fought hard to continue the legacy of Drie Fonteinen. In 1953, Gaston Debelder began blending lambics for a café in the little town of Beersel, Belgium.

After seven years of mellowing, the intricacies of this oude geuze were in full bloom.

Like many gueuze blenders, the family purchased young lambics from larger breweries and then aged and conditioned them themselves prior to blending. When the business was passed on to him, Armand felt so passionate about the quality and control of his product that he began to brew the lambic himself. That changed in 2009, however, when a series of financial disasters brought brewing to a halt. Drie Fonteinen nearly went under, but an outpouring of support from the beer community brought it back from the brink to the thriving *geuzestekerij* (gueuze-blending facility) it is today. So impressive has been the turnaround that new brewing equipment was being installed at the time of writing. This, along with Armand naming an heir to the Drie Fonteinen throne, Michael Blancquaert (a very promising and capable young blender), ensures that the future of this excellent *oude geuze* is bright.

FRESH TASTING CRITIQUE

APPEARANCE: Apricot hue with a vigorous, fluffy, white head; excellent retention. Slight haziness.

SMELL: Intense sour lactic aroma paired with lemon, apple, and peach. Equally dominant funkiness of wet hay, horse blanket, and leather.

TASTE: As with the aroma, the dominant flavors are funk and lactic sourness; both very intense. Accompanying them is a honeylike graininess and strong, bitter phenols.

The fruity esters are even more powerful than the aroma suggests but still take a backseat to the sour funkiness.

MOUTHFEEL: Extremely effervescent and quite dry. No alcohol presence.

OVERALL IMPRESSION: This is an exceedingly complex, delicious beer. Armand has done an amazing job of blending the grainy bitterness of the young with the funky acidity of the old, making this combination an experience in and of itself.

AGING EXPECTATIONS

Like most quality gueuzes, this one is blended to create an integrated, complex beer that has already undergone substantial aging when "fresh." It does not require or demand aging, yet many may find they prefer the profile of a gueuze that has experienced further aging. As it ages, the beer becomes slightly more sour, though less sharp. The funk remains present but is no longer the dominant characteristic. This development allows the subtle oak, fruit, and *sur lie* flavors to emerge, creating a more elegant, delicate beer.

APPEARANCE: Over a period of ten years, this beer darkens slightly, starting at a light orange hue and ending at an apple cider amber. The haze clears completely around year two, though this depends greatly on the pour of this sediment-laden brew. Typically, the carbonation is retained well, showing only a slow decline.

SMELL: After two years, the initial funky barnyard aspects have started to become subdued, but the lactic sourness remains. With these changes, the fruit and oak complexities come forward.

After four years, both the lactic tanginess and brett-induced aroma have sufficiently mellowed, and distinct flavors of tropical fruit interplay with a leather oakiness. A subtle *bière de garde* mustiness emerges.

Bottles older than six years or so display significant vintage-to-vintage variation, but the lactic sourness is substantially tamed, and a musty, cobweb aroma takes center stage alongside a citrusy zest.

TASTE: A couple of years in the cellar results in a slightly restrained sour funkiness, paralleling the aroma. The overall profile is mostly unchanged, just less intense. After nearly four years, however, both the phenolic bitterness and the honey graininess have been greatly reduced, resulting in a more graceful flavor.

By year six, the barnyard flavors have been greatly toned down, there is essentially no phenolic bitterness, and the oak and tropical-fruit flavors, as well as a light mustiness, are quite evident. It's at ten years that any trace of malt has vanished, leaving a beverage almost more like wine than beer. A distinct, soft, lemony character provides a base for a bouquet of delicate, complex flavors.

After a much longer time (20-plus years), excellent-quality gueuzes can create *sur lie* flavors similar to vintage Champagne. The hazelnut and toasted-bread flavors in these gueuzes are some of the most highly prized aspects of vintage beers.

MOUTHFEEL: As the brett slowly consumes the blended young lambic's sugars, the already light mouthfeel becomes even more dry. This occurs in tandem with the reduction in carbonation, resulting in a dry, winelike mouthfeel.

OVERALL IMPRESSION: The *oude geuze* stands up longer to cellaring than just about any other style, and Drie Fonteinen's is one of the best examples of this. Though perfectly enjoyable when first bottled, this beer ages into a mellowed, better-integrated beverage. If you enjoy the subtle grainy sweetness of a young lambic, don't age much beyond a few years. Those who prefer more fruity, oaky characteristics, on the other hand, should age this beer up to five years. If you value the musty nuances and winelike nature of a vintage gueuze, stretch it out to ten years. And finally, those with *extraordinary* patience should hide these away for 20 to 30 years (and please send an invite my way before you open it).

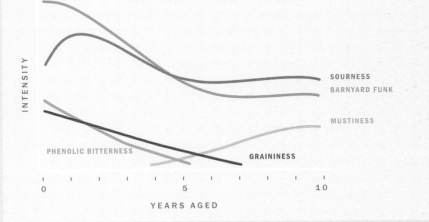

DRIE FONTEINEN OUDE GEUZE AGING PROFILE

INTENSITY

SOURNESS

BARNYARD FUNK

MUSTINESS

PHENOLIC BITTERNESS

GRAININESS

0   5   1 0

YEARS AGED

BROOKLYN BREWERY BLACK CHOCOLATE STOUT

STYLE: Imperial stout

ABV: 10%

BOTTLE SIZE: 12 fl. oz.

HISTORY: "Delicious when newly bottled, but also ages beautifully for years." This is Brooklyn Brewery's own (and accurate) quote for its imperial stout, one of the first brewed in the United States. Founders Steve Hindy and Tom Potter started out selling their beer from the back of a van, and now the company distributes to 25 states and 20 countries. Debuting in 1994, the Black Chocolate Stout owes its coffeelike flavor to a variety of specialty roasted malts, while the beta-balanced Willamette and

Noting that the roastiness and alcohol had mellowed and permitted other flavors to come forward, the panel chose a three-year-old bottle as the peak.

alpha-stacked Fuggle hops take credit for the substantial hopping (51 IBUs). The stout is aged for two months in the bottle prior to release, which helps to soften some rough edges. It's a little confusing, but the product label carries two vintages (e.g. "Winter 08/09") because it is released in October but available until March, spanning two different calendar years.

FRESH TASTING CRITIQUE

APPEARANCE: Jet-black with a one-finger tan-tinged head; low head retention. No sediment.

SMELL: Rich, espresso aroma blended with dark chocolate. A light, resiny English hop presence lingers in the background. Some fusel alcohols, but nothing overwhelming.

TASTE: The main flavor is the same intense roasted malt notes of espresso and bittersweet chocolate present in the nose. The roast is mildly astringent like a strong Italian coffee, with some hop bitterness, but very little hop flavor. Yeast esters are at a minimum. This is a malt-forward beer. It has an alcohol presence that straddles the line between warming and boozy.

MOUTHFEEL: A fair amount of sweetness provides a full mouthfeel despite the alcohol content. Carbonation is at a medium level and helps to cut through the sweetness.

OVERALL IMPRESSION: With the intense roasted flavors and aroma masking many of the secondary aspects, the beer is somewhat one-dimensional. In addition, the alcohol presence strains toward assertiveness.

AGING EXPECTATIONS

This beer begs to be aged. Expect the strong coffee characteristics that overshadow the other components of the beer, as well as the prominent alcohol impression, to mellow. The large malt bill provides some pleasant oxidization characteristics, and the yeast esters develop dried-fruit aspects.

APPEARANCE: Already black as night, the color remains unchanged. The bottle cap proved to be quite secure: the ten-year-old bottle retained about half the carbonation of a fresh bottle. Head retention dropped even lower due to the coagulation of the malt proteins.

SMELL: The bitter, roasted aroma gradually decreases as the beer ages and other flavors come forth to create a more complex taste profile. After only one year, the yeast esters start to show development of notes of raisin and prune, and the alcohol on the nose fades dramatically. The hop aroma, while still detectable at this point (and maybe even more noticeable because of the reduced roasted malt bitterness), is gone for good in later bottles.

Signs of oxidation, in the form of leather and a subtle hazelnut aroma, appear near year two. The dried-fruit esters increase in intensity through the fourth year.

At the five-year mark, however, a dramatic medicinal aroma is evident. The tasting panel was split on whether it was autolysis or some other degradation, but all agreed it overwhelmed all the positive aging flavors. All older bottles carried a similar smell.

TASTE: The somewhat strong alcohol presence of the fresh version fades to a creaminess after the first year and becomes a positive aspect. As with the aroma, after the first year the sweetness of the malt emerges in notes of toffee and treacle just as some of the astringent roasted flavors begin to soften. Bottles at two to three years old exhibit an excellent balance of the two, beautifully showcasing this beer's "black chocolate" name. After about four years the leather begins to transition to a tobacco taste, a good or bad thing depending on the individual.

A taste of wet paper comes up around the two-year mark and gradually increases over time. Though not overwhelming, it becomes disagreeable at around five years. However, this is the same time that medicinal notes develop (again, paralleling the aroma's development), overriding the other aspects of the beer. But this is not unlike what happens to most dark beers as a result of the increased aging rate from the large amount of high-roast malts.

MOUTHFEEL: During the first few years, as the sweet caramel malt flavors develop and the roast fades, the mouthfeel gives the impression of intensifying. The carbonation stays remarkably strong over the years, although it does decrease gradually.

OVERALL IMPRESSION: This beer is a worthwhile candidate for any cellar.

It experiences amazing growth in just a year and continues to improve and develop complexities throughout the next few years. How long to age this beer depends on how much roasted character you desire. If you want an espresso quality, a single year of aging will be enough, but barley wine fans will prefer a three-year-old vintage with its combination of sherry, raisins, and dark chocolate. Thanks to its widespread availability and great price, there's no reason not to have this in your cellar; just be careful not to hold it too long.

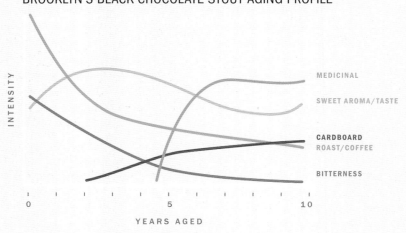

BROOKLYN'S BLACK CHOCOLATE STOUT AGING PROFILE

RODENBACH GRAND CRU

STYLE: Flanders red ale

ABV: 6%

BOTTLE SIZE: 750 mL

HISTORY: Crafted by a brewery active for nearly 200 years, Rodenbach's Grand Cru is considered by most to be the quintessential Flanders red ale. This style, often called the Burgundy of Belgium, is usually a blend of young and oak-aged beer. While the standard Rodenbach red is a 75-25 blend of young-to-aged beer, the Grand Cru flips the ratio, with 66 percent being made up of beer that has been aged at least two years in their legendary

Giving the Grand Cru a few years allows the young beer's sweetness to subside and the fruity sour flavors to come through.

oak port foeders. In 1998, Rodenbach was acquired by Palm Breweries, and though many feared that the Grand Cru's days were numbered, Palm has instead expanded the range of aged reds. We can now enjoy Caractère (aged two years on cherries and raspberries), Vin de Céréale (higher alcohol, three-year-old beer), and vintage-labeled, unblended bottles of Grand Cru filled from specially chosen foeders.

FRESH TASTING CRITIQUE

APPEARANCE: Deep garnet-brown, hefty off-white head settles to a lacy consistency. Very slight haziness.

SMELL: Intensely fruity with cherry and grape in the fore and green apple and citrus lingering in the background. A distinct acidic tang contrasts with subtle oaky vanilla. The young beer's strong malty sweetness contrasts with the acidity of the old.

TASTE: As in the nose, the fruity acidity is big here. There are loads of cherry, berry, and grape as well as a strong lactic sourness. Also notable is a slight acetic (vinegar) presence, but not to the point of being a detriment. The beer has a substantial malty sweetness and mild oakiness. No noticeable hop and minimal alcohol presence.

MOUTHFEEL: The full-bodied sweetness is cut somewhat by the considerable acidity; medium-high carbonation.

OVERALL IMPRESSION: A powerhouse of sweet and sour flavors that demands attention. This combination is immensely enjoyable but masks some of the more delicate features.

AGING EXPECTATIONS

This beer's intense sweetness when young is a major reason to age it. And with its relatively low ABV, the high acidity will enable slow aging. Time will reduce the malty sweetness, letting the acidity and other flavors come forward. Later the acidity rounds off and gives the oxidation-related malts and oak aspects a chance to become more prominent. Because of the pasteurization, the beer will not become any more sour (nor develop any brett notes), although it may initially appear to do so since the contrasting sweetness is reduced.

APPEARANCE: The initial ruby hue lightens over the years to an orangish color. Sadly, but as expected, the head retention and carbonation steadily decline, though there are still some bubbles after a decade.

SMELL: In the first couple of years, the fresh malty aroma fades, which elevates the fruit and acid aspects. After around three years, the cherry aroma mellows slightly, allowing the oxidation-derived malt flavors (toffee and caramel) to come to the fore. Additionally, the oak begins to move forward, but not to a great degree.

Aging a few years further yields a greatly reduced fruit flavor, although what is left has a pleasant dried-fruit profile. The malt is less sweet and comes through aged and like molasses; there is also a tinge of old oak. Overall, the aroma diminishes considerably.

At around ten years, the aroma is hardly detectable, with only a hint of molasses and oak. Also at this age, a mild solvent flavor occurs from the aged acetic acid.

TASTE: The beer seems to become more sour in the first two years as the malty sweetness eases. This fruity sourness is the dominant flavor until the beer is about three years old, at which point the maltiness returns in notes of treacle and bread pudding. While the oak is still lightly obscured, its presence is discernible in the flavors of vanilla and tobacco. Around this time a subtle cardboard taste becomes present, but it's easily overlooked.

At five and six years, aging yields a much more subdued, delicate beer. The fruit is now present only in the notes of dried cranberry and prune, and the malt and oak are the dominant flavors. Just as the aroma foretold, the malt now tastes more roasted, like molasses. The oak and phenolic flavors of vanilla, leather, and tobacco truly shine at this point.

At the decade mark, the beer is greatly mellowed. The flavors are balanced, but they lack the intensity to be thoroughly enjoyable.

MOUTHFEEL: Incredibly thick and sweet when fresh, the Grand Cru has the legs to support it through a long cellaring. A few years cut the sweetness considerably, and after about five years, you'd be hard-pressed to call it full-bodied. However, it isn't until it's about ten years old that it could be considered thin, though it's not unpleasant.

OVERALL IMPRESSION: The Grand Cru undoubtedly improves with age. While delicious fresh, a little time allows the flavors to mellow to a point where they're all present on the stage. How long it should be aged varies greatly among drinkers. Those looking for a still-fruity, sweet beer should age this brew for only a year or two. People who appreciate the dried-fruit and toffee aspects are better off letting it go until four to six years. And although it certainly isn't bad beyond this point, the characteristics that make it great are too subdued to justify additional aging.

RODENBACH GRAND CRU AGING PROFILE

INTENSITY

OAK

SWEETNESS

CARDBOARD
FRUITINESS

0   5   10

YEARS AGED

TRAPPISTES ROCHEFORT 10

STYLE: Belgian quad

ABV: 11.3%

BOTTLE SIZE: 11.2 fl. oz.

HISTORY: One of only seven remaining Trappist monasteries making beer, and certainly one of the most traditional, Rochefort produces three world-class brews, named simply 6, 8, and 10. Having begun brewing operations in 1595, the monastery has certainly had time to hone its craft. The 6 is a delightful dry Dubbel, and the 8, with its dark, malty fruitiness, is fantastic, but it's the mighty 10 that is the superstar of the group. Like many of the dark, very strong Trappist beers, it needs time for its rough edges to smooth, but when they finally do, it's

The monastery's five-year "best by" date is right on, with the beer reaching its full potential at this point.

one of the best. The vintage can be determined by the printed "best by" date code on the label, which is five years after it was bottled. The European dating style is used (where the day precedes the month), so "310716" would indicate a July 31, 2011, bottling date. And being sold in packs of four 11.2-ounce bottles sets you up perfectly for regular tastings to follow its development.

FRESH TASTING CRITIQUE

APPEARANCE: Dark-brown pour with a foaming, off-white head, which quickly dissipates and leaves essentially no trace; noticeable haziness.

SMELL: A malty, colalike sweetness hits first, quickly followed by a strong phenolic bitter presence of pepper, clove, and cinnamon. The yeast is very apparent in notes of rising bread dough. A slight, off-putting metallic aroma pervades.

TASTE: The first sensation is a one-two punch of the same phenolic presence and cola sweetness. This results in a saccharine flavor reminiscent of diet cola. The fresh bread yeastiness remains, accompanied by stewed prunes. A strong, hot alcohol taste pushes the boundary of being tolerable. No hop flavor and only a slight hop bitterness are present.

MOUTHFEEL: Quite dry and when paired with the intense, prickly carbonation, there is again the association of diet cola.

OVERALL IMPRESSION: The 10 offers a variety of interesting aspects. Unfortunately, it's not entirely enjoyable due to a lack of balance between the strong phenols, high carbonation, and powerful alcohol presence.

AGING EXPECTATIONS

When it comes to strong Belgian beers, it's tough to write a better script for aging. As oxidation sets in, the initially harsh phenols and fusels mellow and develop a pleasant complexity. Additionally, the high initial carbonation lessens, which greatly helps in the long run.

APPEARANCE: The 10 lightens mildly over time, ranging from a dark brown when fresh to an amber hue after about ten years. The haze persists until around five years of age. Surprisingly, the head retention follows a bell curve, leading one to wonder if a change in brewing or recipe is the culprit.

SMELL: In the first couple of years the phenolic character greatly subsides, leaving soft notes of tobacco and wood. The maltiness comes forward in a sweet nuttiness, although there's still a cola aspect. At this point, the initial metallic aroma has completely disappeared, and though the booziness is still present, it has mellowed.

After about five years the harsh alcohol presence disappears and the phenols transform into rich vanilla, leather, and tobacco. The maltiness is now like bittersweet chocolate. Hints of dried cherry, fig, and prune abound, and the yeasty bread dough presence is retained.

The aging malt aromas in the eight- to ten-year bottles increase, resulting in hints of toffee and bread pudding and a stronger influence of dried fruit. Remaining flavors have, however, diminished.

TASTE: Through the first five years, the taste profile of the beer follows very closely the development of the aroma. The initially harsh phenols transform into flavors of vanilla, leather, and tobacco, and the booziness mellows dramatically. The dried fruits also develop, and the fresh yeasty bread dough flavor persists.

Beyond five years, however, the taste profile departs dramatically from the aroma. While the nose of even years eight, nine, and ten retains a rich maltiness and fruitiness, the flavor of these bottles falls off and is quite muted — just a trace of what the aroma would lead you to expect. After about ten years, the overall taste is watery, with a stale, dark malt flavor and only the merest suggestion of dried fruit.

MOUTHFEEL: Carbonation is the key player through the years. Initially harsh and working in tandem with the bitter phenols, it makes this beer quite dry when fresh. However,

TRAPPISTES ROCHEFORT 10 (CONTINUED)

as the carbonation reduces and the phenols transform, the beer obtains an apparent sweetening for about six years, after which it thins to the point of being a detriment.

OVERALL IMPRESSION: You would be hard put to find a beer that benefits so greatly from aging. While the phenols and fusels make it harsh and rough when young, these same components provide the building blocks for creating deliciously complex flavors. Those looking to retain some phenolic character should stick to the bottles of between three and four years old, while barley wine fans will certainly appreciate the prominent dried-fruit and toffee-malt flavors of vintages at five to six years old. Given how well it ages, its availability, and relatively low price, Rochefort 10 is my cellar's go-to Belgian quad.

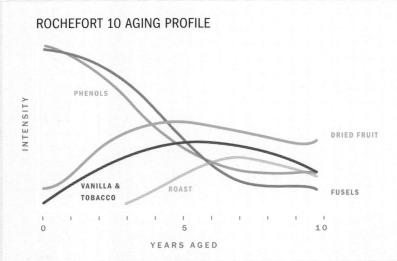

ROCHEFORT 10 AGING PROFILE

ANCHOR BREWING CHRISTMAS ALE

STYLE: Winter spiced ale

ABV: 5.5%

BOTTLE SIZE: 12 fl. oz.

HISTORY: Anchor Brewing Company, established in San Francisco in 1896, is one of the oldest operating breweries in the United States. The original creator of "steam ale," it began brewing its seasonal Christmas Ale in 1975. This dark, spiced ale is unique in that the recipe changes every year. While the base beer remains the same, each vintage is complemented with a new variety of spices, whose specific makeup the brewery chooses to keep a close secret. This beer is recognizable

As the spices meld with aged toffee flavors, this winter spiced ale drinks well at around two years of age.

by its label's signature hand-drawn tree (different every year) by Bay Area artist Jim Stitt, alongside which you'll find the beer's vintage. The ale comes in six-packs as well as 50.7-ounce (1.5-liter) magnums. The label's indication of vintage and the festive large-size bottles suggest that the ale is intended to be aged, and it is a beer that rewards after some cellaring.

FRESH TASTING CRITIQUE

NOTE: *This review is of the most recent version at the time of writing.*

APPEARANCE: Very dark brown with a slight garnet hue; foamy white head that quickly dissipates. Quite clear.

SMELL: Very aromatic with intense perfume notes. Hints of hibiscus and heather mix with the traditional holiday spice blend of clove, nutmeg, ginger, and cinnamon. Slight anise presence as well as subtle nutty malt aroma, which, however, is overshadowed by the other ingredients. No hop or alcohol aromas.

TASTE: The malt flavor takes center stage with notes of dry toasted bread and biscuits. Quite dry without the noticeable tannins that spiced beers often have from the use of overprocessed spice. The perfumed, spicy flavors maintain a strong presence. There is some hop bitterness but no real hop flavor. No noticeable alcohol warming.

MOUTHFEEL: The body is relatively thin, and there is a moderate amount of carbonation.

OVERALL IMPRESSION: An intensely aromatic beer from the spices and various secret ingredients. A pleasant malt taste adds to the complexity despite the relatively low ABV.

AGING EXPECTATIONS

The relatively low alcohol content and residual sugar do not call for aging this beer a long time. The intense aromas, however, suggest that the beer could benefit from a period of mellowing and integrating its various layers, much like with a stew that improves after a night in the fridge.

APPEARANCE: This beer darkened slightly across years, but that could be due to the recipe changes. Head retention, though never strong, steadily declined but was still present at the ten-year mark.

SMELL: While the aroma of each vintage changes based on the spices used each year, it becomes less overpowering and yields to the malt, with an enjoyable balance found at year two. After the third year, the spice aroma has faded and leaves the beer lacking its earlier complexity.

A slight oxidation-induced toffee aroma was present from two to four years but faded quickly after, degenerating into an unpleasant, musty solvent aroma at the five-year mark. All vintages beyond this point were far beyond their prime and had lost their original (and any gained) positive attributes.

TASTE: This beer starts out quite dry but obtains a sweetness from the emerging caramel flavors that peaks at about two years and lasts through year three. This slightly toffee, caramel flavor generally blends well with whatever spices happen to be present. After this year, however, the sweetness and enjoyable biscuit flavors of the malt fade and are replaced by a growing cardboard flavor; the beer becomes quite dull and stale.

Just as we saw with the aroma, an off-putting medicinal, solvent flavor appears at five years. The cardboard flavor continues to develop but is made irrelevant by these other unpleasant aspects. Considering its low alcohol and residual sugars and its use of spices, it is surprising that the beer cellars this well.

MOUTHFEEL: Already thin when fresh, the mouthfeel never sees much improvement. The carbonation is maintained fairly well but helps only to exacerbate the thinness of the ale. After about the three-year mark, the body is reminiscent of diet cola.

OVERALL IMPRESSION: This beer shows some improvement from aging a few years. The main reason to cellar it is to allow the spices (so prominent in a fresh bottle) to integrate with the rest of the beer's components. While the spices smooth, the malt begins to sweeten slightly and hints of toffee appear. Three years seems to be this beer's maximum, and it falls off quickly after that. A good approach is to buy a magnum each year to cellar. That way, every year you'll have a matured version that makes for a perfect spiced winter ale and a great conversation piece at any holiday party.

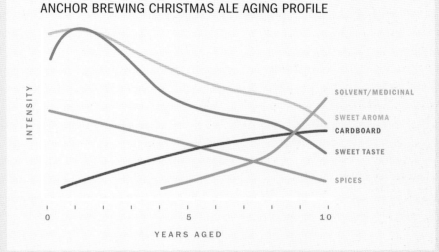

ANCHOR BREWING CHRISTMAS ALE AGING PROFILE

INTENSITY

SOLVENT/MEDICINAL
SWEET AROMA
CARDBOARD
SWEET TASTE
SPICES

0   5   10

YEARS AGED

SCHNEIDER & SOHN AVENTINUS

STYLE: Weizenbock

ABV: 8.2%

BOTTLE SIZE: 16.9 fl. oz.

HISTORY: Aventinus, created in 1907 by the famous Bavarian brewery Schneider & Sohn, lays claim to being the first weizenbock ever brewed. This somewhat obscure German beer style is essentially the merging of the yeast/wheat character of a hefeweizen and the malty richness of a doppelbock. German beer connoisseurs recognized the cellaring potential of this beer long ago, and in 1999 the brewery decided to follow suit. Every year, 240 cases are added to the brewery's "ice cellar" and aged for three years before being released.

Featuring vibrant wine-like esters, this weizenbock peaks at four to five years.

This brewery-aged version is great for cellaring not only because much of the waiting has already been done for you but also because of the optimal conditions in which the beer has been stored. The brewery-aged version comes wrapped in paper that states the vintage. The age of regular bottles can be determined by the YY.DDD date code on the back label. For example, a beer with 11.199 would have been bottled on the 199th day of 2011.

FRESH TASTING CRITIQUE

APPEARANCE: Deep copper-brown with substantial cloudiness from the wheat malt. Pours with a tall, lasting off-white head.

SMELL: Intense aroma of phenols and esters associated with hefeweizen, clove, vanilla, and banana. Stone-fruit esters linger in the background while a thick, malty sweetness interplays with the yeast, resulting in hints of dark candi sugar and caramel. A mild bready note from the wheat malt and slight floral alcohol fusels are also present.

TASTE: Rich melanoidins are prominent up front, with notes of caramel and chocolate. As with the aroma, the yeast gives off dark fruits such as prunes and raisins, clove, vanilla, and banana, while the wheat comes through in a thick bread-dough flavor. Minimal hop bitterness, and no hop flavor; pleasant warming alcohol presence.

MOUTHFEEL: The chewy, wheaty mouthfeel is nicely contrasted by the high carbonation. High residual maltiness of a bock.

OVERALL IMPRESSION: This is an amazingly complex brew that beautifully merges all the various aspects that make doppelbocks and German *Weiss* beers great.

AGING EXPECTATIONS

Aspects such as its high alcohol, rich malt melanoidins, dark-fruit esters, strong phenols, and residual sugars would seem to put this beer forward as an obvious candidate for cellaring. On the other hand, its age-sensitive features like banana esters and wheatiness suggest the opposite. However, experience demonstrates that this beer ages incredibly well, transforming into something unique and unrecognizable when compared to its former self.

APPEARANCE: Aventinus darkens slightly over time, but the major change is the clearing of the wheat cloudiness. After only a year, much of it has cleared, with a fair amount of brown pigment forming at the base of the bottle. Head retention diminishes slowly.

SMELL: The aroma rides a roller coaster of changes during aging. The banana esters that are so prominent in the beginning fade quickly and are completely absent after about year three. The initial fusels evolve into sweet caramel, and the malt melanoidins bring out hints of sherry at three years. Fruit notes of plum, pear, and grape build, reaching a climax in years four to five, after which they weaken and begin to take on more dried-fruit aspects. After about seven years, the dominant aroma is sherry, and much of the earlier complexity is gone. All the while, the clove phenols transform linearly into vanilla and still appear in even a ten-year-old bottle.

TASTE: Following the trend of the aroma, the forefront yeast and wheatiness fade quickly, and what were initially just background flavors come forward. Around year three, sherry flavor develops. The fruity esters evolve into a pleasant grape flavor at around five years due to the gradual degradation of the noble Hallertau hop's beta acids.

After an initial decrease in wheaty/malty flavors, the fusels begin to develop into toffee flavors, and the beer grows in sweetness until about year six, when the thinning residual sugars become noticeable. Beyond seven-plus years the focal point is sherry, and while enjoyable, this starts to become one-dimensional.

MOUTHFEEL: The mouthfeel, too, undergoes massive change over ten years of aging. The initial chewy wheatiness disappears after only one or two years, but the increasingly sweet flavors nicely fill the gap.

SCHNEIDER & SOHN AVENTINUS (CONTINUED)

However, after around year seven, the thinning of the malt is noticeable and becomes a definite drawback of the beer. Carbonation is maintained well over time, and even the ten-year-old bottle opened with a hiss, pouring with a slight head.

OVERALL IMPRESSION: Aventinus is incredible fresh, but it also amply rewards anyone with the patience to cellar it. The tasting panel unanimously agreed it was the favorite vertical because of the fact that every vintage was enjoyable, though each for unique reasons. The beer reaches its peak between years four and five, with all concluding that these are the most complex yet balanced vintages. The stone-fruit esters at this point are vibrant but balanced wonderfully by a host of other flavors. Fans of the wheatier, spicy aspects of the beer will enjoy the younger vintages. Cellarers fond of sherry will appreciate years seven through eight, when that flavor is prominent but still nicely complemented by other aspects.

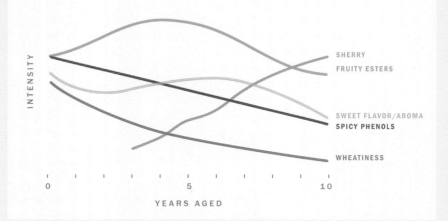

SCHNEIDER'S AVENTINUS AGING PROFILE

INTENSITY

SHERRY
FRUITY ESTERS

SWEET FLAVOR/AROMA
SPICY PHENOLS

WHEATINESS

0   5   10

YEARS AGED

OTHER AGE-WORTHY BEERS
ORVAL

Orval is a unique beer that defies easy style categorization. When fresh, it has
a hop bite and a pleasant grainy sweetness. However, its monk producers pitch
Brettanomyces in each bottle immediately prior to bottling, and though it's
initially undetectable, the brett begins to consume the residual sugars left from
the traditional brewer's yeast after a year or so. This additional fermentation
creates a slight barnyard funkiness and complementary tropical-fruit notes. Age
beyond this point and the malt flavor slowly begins to fade as the brett continues
consuming the residual sugars, and the funky phenols become more prominent.
After about three years, Orval is extremely dry and loaded with so much funkiness
that it will be too unbalanced for most — excluding only the biggest brett fans.

SCHLOSS EGGENBERG SAMICHLAUS

Brewed only once a year on December 6, this 14 percent ABV beer claims to be
the strongest lager in the world. Something like an ultrastrong doppelbock, it is
one of the few lagers found in your average beer cellar. Fermentation takes ten
months to complete, so the youngest bottle you'll find will already be at least a
year old. When drunk young, the beer offers layers of toffee, burnt sugar, and
a hint of chocolate; these, however, are masked by intense fusel alcohol notes
of rum and fruit. After five or so years, the booziness mellows dramatically and
emergent aspects of sherry and raisin begin to mingle with the burnt-sugar
flavors. After ten to fifteen years, this special lager is impressively smooth and
brings notes of stewed plums, tobacco, and Madeira, yet retains enough residual
sugar to provide a solid base for the flavors to stand upon. This is a cellar classic.

ALASKAN BREWING SMOKED PORTER

This full-bodied porter is brewed with alder-smoked malts. The beer has an
impressive amount of residual sugars and when fresh is charged with smoke,
chocolate, and dark fruits (raisin, currant). Weighing in at only at 6.5 percent ABV,
it might not seem at first to be a good cellaring candidate. However, the smoke-
derived phenols act as a preservative, just as a higher level of alcohol would,
permitting the beer to cellar exceptionally well. After three to four years, the
smoke mellows and notes of sherry, fig, and caramel surface. The high residual
sugars stand up for around ten years, after which the beer's body becomes too
thin to justify further aging.

CHAPTER 5

Dark and Cool: Selecting Your Cellar

As with many things, your beer cellar depends on location, location, location. What makes for a proper cellar is worth some serious consideration. With time, money, and effort going into your collection, it makes sense to be selective about where you're going to age it. There are several things to consider, chief of which are temperature, light exposure, humidity, and configuration. But don't worry — a decent cellaring environment can be created in just about any home.

TEMPERATURE

Temperature is going to be the main factor when determining a spot to cellar your beers. Too warm, and your beer will age rapidly; too cold, and the aging processes will slow to a crawl. Although research on the chemistry of beer-cellar temperatures has so far been limited to home enthusiasts like yourself, a good deal has been done regarding the aging of wine. It's been determined that red wine ages optimally at around 55°F (13°C). This temperature allows the various aging processes to take place but at a rate low enough to allow the slow-to-develop flavors from aging to emerge. Aging red wine at temperatures warmer than this causes a drastic increase in the wine's aging (see table 3, page 112).

Table 3: Equivalent age of red wine compared with a wine cellared at 55°F (13°C) for one year

CELLAR TEMPERATURE (DEGREES F/C)	CHEMICALLY EQUIVALENT AGE (YEARS)
59/15	1.2–1.5
73/23	2.1–8.0
91/33	4.1–56

I know what many of you are thinking: so all that beer I've been aging in my closet is ruined!? But don't fret; it's been my experience that the organic matter found in wine and other fruits are much more susceptible to degradation than beer is. Much of this is due to the fact that wine is not cooked like beer is (Mevushal wine aside). This heating process activates the most temperature-sensitive organic processes prior to fermentation, thereby creating a much more stable product than wine. Don't believe me? Look no further than how fast that fruit flavor (which was added post boil) fades out of your favorite fruit-spiked beer.

I've had two bottles of the same beer, same vintage, but one aged at 55°F (13°C) and the other at 70°F (21°C), and though I detected differences, they weren't damning enough to convince me to rush out and buy a $1,000 wine fridge. On the other hand, I've also had two bottles of the same beer, same vintage, one aged at 65°F (18°C) and the other at 85°F (30°C), and the difference was considerable. So while the rate for beer is probably not the same as red wine, it's clear that the rate of aging goes up exponentially with increasing temperatures.

While it's optimal to keep your cellar as close to 55°F (13°C) as possible, what's paramount is that beers are cellared below their fermentation temperature. For ales (most age-worthy beers), that temperature falls in the range of 65 to 73°F (18–23°C). So your cellar should be below 65°F (18°C) to be on the safe side. Each potential chemical process in a beer has an activation temperature it has to reach to be able to start. Hence, exposing a beer to

Use a remote thermostat to track your cellar's temperature.

a temperature higher than where it was fermented will set off all sorts of new flavors and aromas, most of them not very positive.

Another thing to keep in mind related to temperature is that you want to maintain stability. Aging processes in beer like to occur within a specific temperature range. If your cellar temperature swings 10°F (6°C) between night and day or is 45°F (7°C) in winter and 75°F (24°C) in summer, different chemical processes will continually start and stop. This can lead to off flavors due to the processes that started but couldn't finish. An ideal beer cellar will therefore keep a near-constant temperature. And, as a general rule, a stable but slightly higher temperature is preferred over a cooler space that experiences large temperature fluctuations.

LIGHT EXPOSURE

After temperature, the next important consideration is light exposure. The most sensitive component of a beer is the hops. Hoppiness is not only the first thing to go, but it's also the most problematic. UV rays break down the hop compounds to create skunky, "light-struck" flavors. If you've ever had a green-bottled beer that's spent more than a few days under fluorescent liquor-store lights, you've surely tasted this flavor. Clear and green bottles (and blue, for that matter) block essentially none of the damaging UV light, while brown bottles block most, though not all. Skunk is never a good flavor, and given a few years, even a brown bottle exposed to light (natural or electric) will start to get skunky. Because of this, avoid decorative display wine racks. They may look great, but their exposure to ambient light is simply going to ruin your beer.

HUMIDITY

Although a major concern in a wine cellar, humidity is more of a minor issue with beer cellars. The wine cellar humidity issue comes from trying to keep corks from drying out. Luckily, the percentage of beers with a cork is pretty small, though most respectable cellars will have a few. Some conscientious breweries cover their corks in plastic, foil, or even wax to help keep them from drying out, and a few even go so far as a cork-and-cap combo. For exposed corks, if the relative humidity in your space is naturally above 55 percent, I wouldn't worry too much about it. Below that, you have a few options. The cheapest approach is to buy bottle wax off the Internet and coat the exposed cork. Depending on your cellar arrangement, you could also get a humidifier, but that can get pricey. A third option is to lay your corked bottles on their side, allowing the beer to contact the cork and thereby keep it moist. However, laying a bottle on its side opens up a whole new can of worms; for more, see Bottle Orientation on page 118.

Ullage

With too much time in a dry environment, a cork will dry out to the point of allowing a bottle's liquid to evaporate. The amount of liquid lost via evaporation is referred to as ullage, and this is a critical factor when thinking about a beer's aging potential. Any liquid volume lost is replaced by ambient oxygen, which accelerates the aging process of a beer. When considering the purchase of very old bottles, be sure to pay close attention to their ullage. Also, when placing corked beers in your cellar, it's a good idea to mark the bottle's initial liquid level.

With the preceding in mind, corkless beers should be stored upright. Orientation of bottle-conditioned corked beers differs according to cellar. In my cellar, the humidity sometimes drops to around 30 percent in the winter, so I wax my exposed corks but keep all the bottles upright. The wax greatly slows the rate of the cork drying, but is still somewhat oxygen

Lambics showing severe ullage.

permeable, and does not entirely stop the drying process. If the humidity were that low year-round, I would most likely lay my bottle-conditioned, corked beers on their sides.

CELLAR CONFIGURATIONS

Considering all this, the answer to "Where should I cellar my beer?" will vary depending on your situation. I am fortunate enough to have an insulated, below-grade crawl space that maintains a temperature between 55 and 65°F (13 and 18°C) year-round. This near-ideal temperature arrangement doesn't cost me a dime of electricity. Plus, the fact that it's a crawl space means it's entirely dark. Best of all, its difficult, hatch-door access actually helps since the beers are out of sight and therefore out of mind (somewhat), giving me the strength to allow them to mature. For all these reasons, I think crawl spaces, basements, and root cellars make the best beer cellars.

If you're not lucky enough to have a storage space like this, not to worry. The next best option, though the most expensive, would be to invest in a wine refrigerator. They're able to maintain almost perfect temperature control and cut out light exposure. Unfortunately, they're not cheap, running anywhere between $100 for a small dorm-size unit up to a few grand for large, fancy double-door units. The key thing to consider is the shelving. Many units are designed for horizontal wine storage, and you have to make sure that the shelving can be removed (or easily modified) to accommodate upright bottle

Waxing a beer can prevent its seal from drying out.

Old refrigerators are a cheap (though not energy-friendly) alternative to decorative refrigerated wine units.

storage. Also keep in mind that the mechanical refrigeration will dramatically dry the air out, and horizontal storage or waxing is necessary for any exposed-cork beers stored for more than a year.

Refrigerated wine units, though ideal, are not required. I have had many great 30-year-old beers that were aged in cabinets and closets. Most people's homes are kept around 70°F (21°C), which avoids reaching above the fermentation temperature of most beer. On top of that, a cabinet or closet has the advantage of shutting out light. If going with this option, be sure to find a place in the interior of your home free from daily temperature swings. Additionally, it's a good idea to put the beers in a cooler or Styrofoam box to somewhat isolate them from temperature fluctuations.

In the closet or cabinet arrangement, humidity will obviously be the same as in your house, so keep that in mind when considering how to store your corked beers. Also remember not to set your thermostat back when you're on vacation, since a week at 85°F (29°C) could essentially cook your cellar.

Bottle Orientation

Horizontal vs. vertical bottle orientation is a hot debate in the vintage beer world. While it's long been customary to store wine on its side, wine has advantages that beer doesn't share, the first being a relative lack of sediment. Since an aging beer accumulates a fair amount of sediment over time, then if stored horizontally, much of it will pour out into your glass, unless you put the bottle upright far in advance of serving.

Bottled wine's other advantage is its (near) lack of headspace. The headspace in a bottle of beer contains oxygen, which is a cause for concern. When stored on its side, the surface area exposed to the headspace is much larger, which accelerates oxidation. However, if a beer is bottle-conditioned, the yeast and its secondary fermentation will consume most of the headspace's oxygen, helping to counteract this tendency.

Many proponents of horizontal bottle orientation also claim that the more exposed the sediment is, the better the secondary conditioning. Beers laid on their side have a much larger sediment surface area than upright bottles. However, for most beers the secondary conditioning of the yeast is done in the first year, thus negating this attribute for long-term storage. Lambic and other sour beers, on the other hand, can experience yeast activity for multiple years, perhaps providing a convincing argument for laying these types of beers on their side for at least the first few years.

If your only option is storing beer in a closet, keep the bottles in an insulated box to protect against daily temperature swings.

CHAPTER 6

How to Manage Your Cellar

When you first begin to accumulate bottles in your cellar, it seems simple enough to keep a mental inventory of your stash. After all, each bottle was carefully chosen and not likely to slip your mind. But as your cellar grows, it becomes difficult to remember what, and particularly how old, each beer is. Enter cellar management, a vital key to successful beer aging.

Why track your beers? Well, consider what could happen if you didn't. I know a handful of cellarers who prefer to "forget" what they're aging and so don't keep a log of their beers. Their theory is that this helps their patience and has the added benefit of their being surprised at what they've got when combing through their collection. The drawback to this approach, and the main reason to keep a cellar log, is to ensure you don't let your beers go past their prime. There is nothing worse than finding a stash of coffee stouts that you wanted to age for six months, three years later.

When entering a beer in your log, it's also a good idea to record your tasting notes alongside. It might be hard to believe, but it is easy to forget how a beer you opened just a few months ago tasted, especially as your cellar grows. So after enjoying a bottle, jotting down a few simple notes indicating whether it was at its prime, still too young, or possibly past its peak will be invaluable later on. Even better, these brief descriptions will help to track how a beer, and to an extent its style, progresses, adding to your ever-growing cellaring knowledge.

How Much Is Enough?

When buying a beer for aging, it's always good to buy in quantity. Purchasing a six-pack (or more) allows you to taste a beer periodically and track how it develops. Experimenting like this is invaluable for gaining an empirical understanding of beer aging. If buying that many bottles isn't always feasible, it's a good idea to purchase at least two and drink one fresh to get an idea of the optimal aging period. Sometimes (and I've been there many times) a beer's rarity and cost allow for only one bottle. In that case, relying on what friends or online tasters have said can help you determine the best time to open the bottle.

Now if I have learned anything in the world of cellaring beer it's that everyone, and I mean everyone, seems to have a different take on the best way to track and manage their collection. Some work with detailed spread-sheets while others stick to the old pen and paper. And an ever-growing number of cellarers are using online methods to easily track their hoard.

The best method in the end is the one that you're most likely to maintain. For a time, I tracked my cellar on a spreadsheet but found that I wasn't always dutiful about logging beers in and out — the computer wasn't fired up, my work-from-home wife was in the middle of editing her music, I couldn't bear to look at Excel for another minute after work — the list of excuses can get long. But after twice going through the disappointment of realizing I'd already drunk the bottle I was looking for, I opted for the old-school pen and paper journal. I have it right at my cellar door, so whenever a beer goes in or out, there's no excuse not to record it. Everyone operates differently, though, so review the various options below to determine which one is right for you.

PAPER JOURNAL

Call me a romantic, but using the good old paper journal to track my cellar just feels right. After all, aging beer, which harks back to ancient Belgian monasteries and the cobweb-strewn brewery cellars of London, has always been logged this way. Something as simple as a three-ring binder should get the job done.

The sample page below shows the fields I feel are necessary to manage your cellar. I keep the columns to a minimum to allow for quick scanning. Notes are limited to short thoughts on how the beer was drinking, and they should always be dated.

When organizing the journal, it's a good idea to have a separate section for each style. This is because you'll often know what type of beer you want (barley wine, for example), it's just a matter of choosing which bottle. This could seem clumsy when you start your cellar since you might have 10 pages to log 10 beers, but after a while this layout will make for a more manageable notebook.

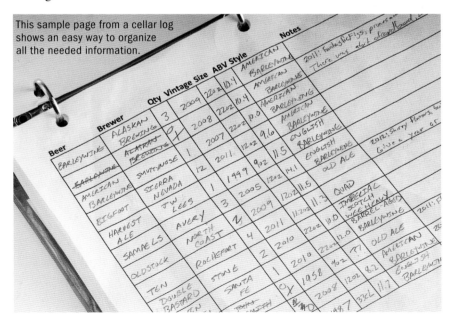

This sample page from a cellar log shows an easy way to organize all the needed information.

A drawback of the paper journal reveals itself when you buy a large amount of a certain beer. If you have a case, or even a six-pack, there is a lot going on in the "Quantity" box, and the "Notes" column can get quite crowded. Additionally, the chronological nature of entries isn't always conducive to easy tracking of a specific beer that you have many vintages of. For example, my various bottles of Thomas Hardy's Ale are spread out over a few pages. Like everything in this world, nothing's perfect.

How Old Is This Bottle?

When it's time to enter a beer in your logbook, it is sometimes difficult to determine the age. Though some brewers are conscientious enough to display the vintage right on the label, more often than not you'll have to employ various tricks to determine just how old the beer is.

Many breweries print some sort of freshness date code on the bottle or packaging. The Fresh Beer Only! website (www.sites.google.com/site/freshbeeronly) is a huge help in deciphering the often bewildering codes.

For beers without freshness dating, the best option is to check out the Alcohol and Tobacco Tax and Trade Bureau (TTB) website. The TTB keeps a database of all beer labels it has ever approved (www.ttbonline.gov/coloasonline/publicsearchcolasbasic.do). Simply searching a brewery's name will yield all its approved labels and associated approval dates. Since most breweries make at least small changes to their labels year to year, finding the one that matches your bottle will tell you what date it was approved, supplying you with a window of when it was brewed.

If nothing else, you can always ask the store's beer manager about the beer's age. Many shops keep records of when beers arrive.

A big thanks to the brewers that display a bottle's vintage.

SPREADSHEET

Although the paper journal has the advantage of accessibility, the benefit of a spreadsheet is its ability to quickly sort a cellar by any field. Let's say you want to know which beer you have the most of (useful for a tasting party) or you want to see only your large-format, magnum-style bottles (also useful for tasting parties); either can be done with the click of the mouse. Moreover, if you decide you want to add, remove, or edit any of the fields, you can easily do so.

After some experience with this method, a drawback I found was that it's not so easy to share your list with guests. It's much easier to toss someone a notebook to choose a beer from than have them sit in front of your computer, or worse, spill beer on your laptop.

If going this route, it's worthwhile to create your spreadsheet using Google Docs (http://docs.google.com). If you're not familiar with it, Google Docs allows users to create spreadsheets and word-processing documents similarly to Excel or Word. However, they have the advantage that they can be viewed and edited online. This means you can access your inventory anywhere (particularly useful at liquor stores) as well as share it with friends online. Choose to make it visible to anyone, or password-protect it.

CELLAR APPS

While they may lack romanticism, there is a growing number of methods to track your cellar on a phone or tablet. These options aim to offer you the accessibility of a paper journal but the electronic advantages of a spreadsheet. With rapid development in the past few years, interfaces are quickly becoming the go-to management platform for many cellarers out there.

Two popular options are the website CellarHQ (www.cellarhq.com) and the iPhone app Brew Vault. Brew Vault is the more versatile of the two. In it, just about every field you could ever want (and a few you'll never use) are available and, as a bonus, the vast majority of beers are pre-populated, meaning you just have to search for them and all the information (ABV, brewery, etc.) comes in preloaded. On top of that, there is also a notes section to track your tastings. Many competing apps (including droid versions) exist, but Brew Vault seems to be the most comprehensive.

CellarHQ lacks some of the bells and whistles of Brew Vault, but it does have the advantage of being free. Plus, it can be accessed by computer, not just your mobile device. It requires the creation of an account, and once logged in you can add beers to your virtual cellar based upon pre-populated lists. The usual fields — style, ABV, quantity, vintage — are all there, but the ever-important "notes" section isn't. Another downside is that once you drink a beer, it's forever gone from your log, which is a real issue for me since I regularly go back to look at thoughts I had on past beers.

Outstanding Vintage-Beer Bars

The pleasures of vintage beer don't have to be limited to drinking only what you age yourself. Luckily, there are a handful of bar owners out there who had the foresight to cellar beer long before most of us were even aware of the concept. I offer here a brief list of bars known far and wide for their attention to vintage beer. There are certainly more around, and new ones pop up regularly, but these are a few with the deepest cellars.

TORONADO

547 Haight Street
San Francisco, CA 94117
415-863-2276
www.toronado.com

Dave Keene opened Toronado's doors in 1987 on the once-notorious Haight Street in downtown San Francisco and started aging beer in the bar's basement that same year. Nondescript and easy to miss, the place is tucked between a pizzeria and a sausage joint, but it offers a heap of vintage goodies to anybody who manages to track it down. Known for its expansive selection and rock-bottom prices, Toronado boasts a large local following, but also plays host to plenty of thirsty beer tourists on pilgrimage.

Though the atmosphere is a little suggestive of a dive bar, one glance at the trophy collection of empty three-liter bottles lining the walls makes it apparent that the place takes its beer very seriously. The bartenders are gruff and none too eager to discuss the beers, but they obviously know their craft. Things get hopping at night,

The Bull & Bush's recent renovation cleared the way for more cellar space.

especially on the weekends, so a weekday lunchtime visit is optimal for those wanting to analyze and enjoy the bar's cellared offerings.

Though a vintage keg or two may occasionally pop up on their 40-plus tap list, the bulk of aged beers are located on the bottle list. Ask the bartender (*nicely*) for the list, since it's kept behind the bar. Amazingly, most beers on the bottle list are available for takeout, though a few of the very rare items are now for on-premise consumption only — since bottles started showing up on eBay. Prices are beyond reasonable, especially considering how expensive a city San Francisco is. Bar manager Steve Bruce says, "These are great beers; we're not going to gouge people. I want to price them where people can enjoy them."

ON THE VINTAGE MENU when I visited were an '07 Rodenbach Grand Cru, a '10 Lost Abbey Cable Car and an '08 Panil Sour Barriquée.

THINGS TO KNOW BEFORE YOU GO: Cash only, ATM available. No food service, though you can bring your own in. Rosamunde Sausage Grill, located next door, is highly recommended.

BULL & BUSH BREWERY
4700 Cherry Creek Drive South
Denver, CO 80246
303-759-0092
www.bullandbush.com

Soon after twin brothers Dean and Dale Peterson opened the Bull & Bush in 1971, it established itself as a staple of the Denver beer scene. But it wasn't until sons Erik and David took

The Falling Rock's cellar is actually a converted elevator shaft.

over that the bar was elevated to world-class status. Brewing operations began in the early 1990s, and the brewery has since won numerous awards, thanks largely to their house-aged vintage beers. In addition to crafting their own cellar-worthy brews, they've slowly amassed beers from around the world for the bar's vintage list.

The bar is straight up old-school British tavern. Its authentic warped copper bar and ancient fireplace were actually transported from defunct English pubs. The looming dark timbers, nook booths, and antique dartboard provide the perfect backdrop for enjoying a vintage ale. The brothers put on minifestivals throughout the year, typically including special vintage kegs that you won't find anywhere else.

Outside these festivals, the vintage stuff is often limited to their bottle selection, which is kept on a separate list (a book, really). After a 2012 renovation that doubled their cellar size, the list grew to around 120 bottles, and the brothers feel confident that they can maintain it. Erik Peterson said, "Most people buy bottles. I buy cases. Always." A wiser man I've never met.

ON THE VINTAGE MENU when I visited were an '03 De Dolle Stille Nacht, an '05 Drie Fonteinen Oude Kriek, a '99 Thomas Hardy's Ale, and an '88 J.W. Lees Harvest Ale.

THINGS TO KNOW BEFORE YOU GO: Full kitchen available. Not all listed vintage offerings are always in stock on-site, so have a few choices in mind.

FALLING ROCK TAPHOUSE

1919 Blake Street
Denver, CO 80202
303-293-8338
http://fallingrocktaphouse.com

One of the original spots in Denver's bar-hopping Lodo district, Falling Rock Taphouse successfully caters to both the young, on-the-prowl crowd and serious beer drinkers. Luckily, they serve the latter very well and the pub crawlers help pay the bills and keep beer prices reasonable. When Chris Black opened the bar in 1997, he immediately decided to set beers aside for aging when he spotted cases of 1994 Thomas Hardy's Ale on his distributor's list. The collection has grown mightily and is stored in an old elevator shaft below the bar.

Set back from busy Blake Street, a pleasant patio fronts the expansive, two-story bar. Inside, the atmosphere is cozy and dark with lots of booths and couches. The place is busy with the party crowd on weekend nights and before, during, and after baseball games, so weekday nights or weekend afternoons are the best times for reflective beer drinking. The joint goes absolutely bonkers with people during the week of the annual Great American Beer Festival, but in a good way.

Of its 69 taps, there are always a few vintage offerings, as Black particularly likes how beer ages in kegs. Ask a bartender or server for the bottle list, which contains an entire section of vintage beer. Prices are pretty reasonable, but can get up there for some of the rarer stuff.

ON THE VINTAGE MENU when I visited were a '97 Bridgeport Old Knucklehead, a '99 Fuller Vintage Ale, and a '94 Thomas Hardy's Ale.

THINGS TO KNOW BEFORE YOU GO: Full kitchen available. Vintage beers often served at refrigerator temperature, so allow for warm-up time when ordering. If you park on the street, don't let your meter run out as Denver meter maids are particularly attentive.

EBENEZER'S RESTAURANT & PUB

44 Allen Road
Lovell, ME 04051
207-925-3200
www.ebenezerspub.net

Chris and Jen Lively opened Ebenezer's Pub, in the little town of Lovell in western Maine, in 2001 to escape the hustle and bustle of the Los Angeles scene. With a population of 974 and the nearest airport a one-and-a-half-hours drive away, they certainly got what they wanted. You'd never guess that this bar, located as it is on the fringe of a golf course in what looks like a barn, houses one of the most impressive cellars in the world.

When its doors first opened, the focus was on food, with a few solid Belgian beers. But as time passed, the Livelys' selection of cellared beers grew, as did the buzz about the place. Now, more than a decade later, Ebenezer's has 35 beers on tap, including many vintage choices.

However, the real treasure is the basement cellar. Through diligent stockpiling and numerous trips overseas, the Livelys' collection has grown into the thousands and contains incredibly rare gems (30-plus-year gueuzes, anyone?) that you'd be hard-pressed to find anywhere else this side of the Atlantic.

The pub itself is rather small and can feel full with a crowd of only 20 or so. While the beer geeks have a definite presence, the regular local crowd provides a refreshing authenticity that elevates the experience above that at so many other East Coast beer bars. As a bonus, the food far outdistances your standard pub grub, making Ebenezer's a true beercation destination.

ON THE VINTAGE MENU when I visited were a '90 Cantillon Classic Gueuze, an '05 De Struise Pannepot Grand Reserva, an '08 Black Albert, and an '07 Fantôme Santé.

THINGS TO KNOW BEFORE YOU GO: Hours of operation are sporadic; always call ahead before making the trek out there. Reservations are strongly recommended. Some vintage offerings are available only when the owners are present. Taxi service is not available; the nearest lodging is two miles away (check the website for info).

CAFE KULMINATOR
Vleminckveld 32
Antwerp, Belgium
+32-3-232-45-38

A 10-year-old Chimay Grande Réserve started it all. The owners, husband and wife Dirk van Dyck and Leen Boudewijn, tried this beer back in the 1970s and enthusiastically set about collecting and aging the huge amount of Belgian goodies the rest of us can now enjoy at their bar. Almost 40 years later, some of their original 1970s-era bottles still appear in their monstrous tome of a bottle list.

Located on a quiet backstreet among the Gothic masterpieces of Antwerp, the Kulminator's exterior is so perfectly ordinary, you could walk by the place day after day and have no idea of the treasures inside. The interior is dark and cozy, and you're greeted by only a smattering of communal tables and a tiny two-person bar. With classical music quietly playing, the random calling of the cuckoo clocks, candles burning, and shelves upon shelves of beer, the mood is perfectly set for knocking some dust off a few ancient beer bottles.

Some 800 beers make up their extensive menu, and they're amazingly well priced considering the age and rarity of the gems to be had. Your biggest problem will be finding enough time to taste all the "must-tries" on the list. You could easily spend a few days here, interspersing your drinking sessions with visits to Antwerp's sights. The place gets pretty full Friday

The Kulminator's tiny bar is no indication of its massive cellar of vintage Belgian beer.

and Saturday nights, so arrive early to nab a seat.

ON THE VINTAGE MENU when I visited were an '86 Chimay Grande Réserve, a '79 Westvleteren Red Cap, an '11 De Struise Kabert, and a '99 De Troch Gueuze.

THINGS TO KNOW BEFORE YOU GO: Hours of operation are sporadic; closed Sundays, otherwise open late afternoon/early evening. Food is limited to cheese and cured meats. Cash only.

BRICK STORE PUB

125 East Court Square
Decatur, GA 30030
404-687-0990
www.brickstorepub.com
Located in Decatur, only about a 15-minute drive from downtown Atlanta, the Brick Store Pub is known for having ". . . no televisions, no neon, no obnoxious music and no major domestic beers." Instead of the stereotypical American bar, it's a place where conversation rules over ESPN and beer is served only if it's worthy of such. The management obviously takes their product seriously. So, when the pub's owners took an '04 trip to

Belgium that included a stopover to Antwerp's famous Kulminator bar, known worldwide for its cellar, no one was surprised when they returned and decided to start a cellar of their own.

Brick Store's "Upstairs Belgian Beer Bar" (kind of a bar-within-a-bar) has elevated the pub to its now legendary status, housing a walk-in cooler that contains 700+ vintage beers ranging from Trappist verticals to rare lambics, plus a healthy number of American one-off specialties. Though their hoard is massive, they don't advertise its existence to avoid depleting it too quickly.

Meander through the front patio into the bricked interior and past the horseshoe-shaped bar fronted by 17 carefully chosen taps; then head upstairs to find the infamous bar and ask for the vintage list. If things are slow, they sometimes let customers choose their own beer from the walk-in: a real treat for those of us who could gawk at shelves of bottles all day.

ON THE VINTAGE MENU when I visited were an '05 De Dolle Oerbier Reserva, an '02 Left Hand Widdershins, and an '05 Fuller's Vintage Ale.

THINGS TO KNOW BEFORE YOU GO: Some "special" beers not always on the tap list; be sure to ask. Limited parking out front, but the MARTA train station only 50 yards away. Full kitchen.

BROUWER'S CAFE

400 North 35th Street
Seattle, WA 98103
206-267-2437
http://brouwerscafe.blogspot.com

Any self-respecting beer fan in the Pacific Northwest has heard of Seattle's legendary beer store, Bottleworks, which is particularly well-known for the fact that it regularly offers vintage beer for sale on its shelves. After years of success, store owners Matt Bonney and Matt Vandenberghe decided to make the jump into the restaurant scene and opened Brouwer's Café. Much like Bottleworks, the café has seen great success, in no small part due to their carefully chosen cellared beer selection.

Located in the hip and quirky Fremont neighborhood, it's easy to miss the wordless sign of a Belgian Lion silhouette. Once inside, though, it's anything but understated, with a massive two-story atrium centered around an expansive 64-tap bar. Add that to a top-end food selection and some of the most knowledgeable servers in the industry, and you can truly appreciate how far the beer-bar scene has come in the past few years.

Vintage beer makes a regular appearance on tap, and an extensive bottle selection is found within its beer menu. In addition, Brouwer's hosts festivals throughout the year; many include vintage kegs, most notably the Hard Liver Barleywine Festival in March.

Soleil de Minuit, a lambic steeped in Swedish cloudberries, made specifically for Akkurat by Cantillon.

ON THE VINTAGE MENU when I visited were an '09 Cascade Kriek, an '08 Hair of the Dog Fred FTW, and an '07 Drie Fonteinen Hommage.

THINGS TO KNOW BEFORE YOU GO: 21 and over only. Website list regularly updated.

AKKURAT RESTAURANT & BAR

Hornsgatan 18
Stockholm 118 20, Sweden
+46-08-644-00-15
www.akkurat.se

Sweden doesn't typically come to mind when you think of beercation destinations. After all, as recent as 1990, the entire country boasted only 13 breweries, and even now all beer has to be bought through state-controlled liquor stores. But hidden inside this slice of Scandinavia is what many consider the best vintage beer bar in the world.

Located on the ground floor of a stark, modern building, Akkurat opened its doors in 1995. Not even a year had passed before operator Sten Isaksson began building his world-renowned cellar collection in the basement. While the focus was initially on Belgian beer, particularly lambics, it has grown to include nearly 500 different beers (and multiple cases of most) from all over the globe. However, it wasn't until sour-beer buffs discovered their Soleil de Minuit that Akkurat gained worldwide recognition. This cloudberry Cantillon lambic was made solely for the bar, and many consider it to be the best lambic ever brewed.

Step into the dark wood interior with its tiled ceilings and you'll immediately be reminded of an authentic Belgian brown café. Settle down with the extensive bottled beer menu that includes some of the rarest vintage beers in the world; entire vacations could be centered around its exploration. As a bonus, when Akkurat isn't too busy, buying a few beers off the menu may persuade the bartender to offer you a cellar tour — a trip you certainly won't forget.

ON THE VINTAGE MENU when I visited were an '00 Drie Fonteinen Malvasia Rosso, a '96 Cantillon Vigneronne, and an '08 Narke Kaggen! Stormakts Porter.

THINGS TO KNOW BEFORE YOU GO: High taxes in Sweden make drinking pricey and Akkurat is no exception; vintage bottles range from $20 to $120. Full kitchen. Live music on Sundays.

MONK'S CAFE

264 South 16th Street
Philadelphia, PA 19102
215-545-7005
http://monkscafe.com

When it comes to Monk's Café, "necessity" is owed much of the credit for its famous cellar. Part-owner and beer geek celebrity Tom Peters first started cellaring beer for just this reason. It all started with him carrying Chimay Grande Réserve in 1985, much to the delight of his customers. But a few years later, the bottles of Chimay "Blue" they were receiving tasted much different, and not in a good way. "Turns out the bottles we had been initially getting were aged two years in a warehouse before they even reached us." So, Peters started aging his Chimay in house, selling both the fresh and the two-year-old bottles (and for only about 50 cents more). People were sold.

Over the years, Monk's cellar grew and began to reach legendary proportions among beer connoisseurs. In fact, Peters was they were selling the beer much faster than he could age it. It was then decided that beers would be held, but only periodically included on the list, to stretch out the supply. Vintage items are limited to those on the menu, but you'll always find some, and they are always exceptional.

The bar itself is very reminiscent of a quaint Belgian café with fabric walls and various antique Belgian beer signs. When visiting Philly, Monk's should be any beer lover's first stop on the list.

ON THE VINTAGE MENU when I visted were an '05 Dogfish Head World Wide Stout, an '08 Cantillon Classic Gueuze, and an '06 De Dolle Oerbier Special Reserva.

THINGS TO KNOW BEFORE YOU GO: Full kitchen. Can get very crowded during the evenings. Very limited street parking.

DELILAH'S

2771 North Lincoln Avenue
Chicago, IL 60614
773-472-2771
www.delilahschicago.com

Abandon all preconceived notions when you enter Delilah's. When a DJ isn't spinning records, punk music rings throughout the air, Miller High Life bottles are on special for $1, and Godzilla is playing on the tube. Oh, and there is a menu with some of the finest vintage beer in the United States. When owner Mike Miller built his bar in 1993, he did it with himself as the target customer. "My bar is going to have the things I like," he says. "I'm the target customer and I like vintage beer and Godzilla movies, so that's what we're going to have."

Like many, Miller was inspired to start his own beer cellar after a trip to Antwerp's Cafe Kulminator in the early '90s. Luckily for those of us on the other side of the bar, he took their same approach to buying beers to cellar in bulk, ensuring that there would be plenty still available when bottles began to peak years later.

Inside the gritty, dark interior, one can't help gawking at the more than 600 bottles of whiskey that line multiple shelves above the bar. The vintage list is spread across the regular beer menu and the "Rare and Vintage" list, both of which are kept behind the bar. And every December during the bar's Vintage Beer Festival, it brings out the best of the best for those who are lucky enough to attend. This event is certainly the best of its kind in the United States, if not the world.

ON THE VINTAGE MENU when I visited were an '07 De Ranke Pere Noel, an '07 Goose Island Bourbon County Brand Stout, and an '03 Bigfoot.

THINGS TO KNOW BEFORE YOU GO: Gets very busy during festivals and Friday/Saturday nights. No food, but you can bring your own.

Other Notable Vintage-Beer Bars

Bittercreek Alehouse, Boise, Idaho

The Farmhouse, Emmaus, Pennsylvania

Gramercy Tavern, New York, New York

Humpy's Great Alaskan Alehouse, Anchorage, Alaska

The Porter Beer Bar, Atlanta, Georgia

Rustico, Alexandria, Virginia

Twisted Spoke, Chicago, Illinois

Le Bier Circus, Brussels, Belgium

De Heeren Van Liederkercke, Denderleeuw, Belgium

In de Verzekering tegen de Grote Dorst, Eizeringen, Belgium

References

The scientific and cultural writings devoted to vintage beers are few. Although many studies have been conducted on the "staling" of light lagers, very little research has been done on the aging effects of higher-alcohol ales and lagers. Beer books often mention vintage beer only fleetingly. However, as interest in high-quality beer grows, so does the study of how it is made and maintained. What follows is the literature that was useful to me in writing this book, and worthwhile reading for anyone interested in exploring vintage beer beyond this book.

McGee, Harold. *On Food and Cooking*, rev. ed. Scribner, 2004.

Oliver, Garrett, ed. *The Oxford Companion to Beer*. Oxford University Press, 2012.

Pandell, Alexander J. "How Temperature Affects the Aging of Wine." *Alchemist's Wine Perspective*, no. 1 (November 1996). www.wineperspective.com/STORAGE%20TEMPERATURE%20&%20AGING.htm

Sparrow, Jeff. *Wild Brews*. Brewers Publications, 2005.

Vanderhaegen, Bart, Hedwig Neven, Hubert Verachtert, and Guy Derdelinckx. "The Chemistry of Beer Aging: A Critical Review." *Food Chemistry* 95, no. 3 (2006): 357–81.

Vanderhaegen, Bart, Filip Delvaux, Luk Daenen, Hubert Verachtert, and Freddy R. Delvaux. "Aging Characteristics of Different Beer Types." *Food Chemistry* 103, no. 2 (2007): 404–12.

Webb, Tim, Chris Pollard, and Siobhan McGinn. *Lambicland*, 2nd ed. Cogan & Mater, 2010.

BEER SCORESHEET

Judge Name (print) _____

Judge BJCP ID _____

Judge Email _____
Use Avery label # 5160

Category # _____ **Subcategory (a-f)** _____ **Entry #** [_____]

Subcategory (spell out) _____
Special Ingredients: _____

Bottle Inspection: ☐ Appropriate size, cap, fill level, label removal, etc.

Comments _____

BJCP Rank or Status:

☐ Apprentice   ☐ Recognized   ☐ Certified
☐ National   ☐ Master   ☐ Grand Master __
☐ Honorary Master ☐ Honorary GM   ☐ Mead Judge
☐ Provisional Judge ☐ Rank Pending

Non-BJCP Qualifications:

☐ Professional Brewer ☐ Beer Sommelier ☐ Non-BJCP
☐ Certified Cicerone ☐ Master Cicerone
☐ Sensory Training   ☐ Other _____

Aroma (as appropriate for style)   _____ /12
Comment on malt, hops, esters, and other aromatics

_____
_____
_____
_____
_____

Descriptor Definitions (Mark all that apply):

☐ **Acetaldehyde** – Green apple-like aroma and flavor.

☐ **Alcoholic** – The aroma, flavor, and warming effect of ethanol and higher alcohols. Sometimes described as *hot*.

☐ **Astringent** – Puckering, lingering harshness and/or dryness in the finish/aftertaste; harsh graininess; huskiness.

☐ **Diacetyl** – Artificial butter, butterscotch, or toffee aroma and flavor. Sometimes perceived as a slickness on the tongue.

☐ **DMS (dimethyl sulfide)** – At low levels a sweet, cooked or canned corn-like aroma and flavor.

☐ **Estery** – Aroma and/or flavor of any ester (fruits, fruit flavorings, or roses).

☐ **Grassy** – Aroma/flavor of fresh-cut grass or green leaves.

☐ **Light-Struck** – Similar to the aroma of a skunk.

☐ **Metallic** – Tinny, coiny, copper, iron, or blood-like flavor.

☐ **Musty** – Stale, musty, or moldy aromas/flavors.

☐ **Oxidized** – Any one or combination of stale, winy/vinous, cardboard, papery, or sherry-like aromas and flavors.

☐ **Phenolic** – Spicy (clove, pepper), smoky, plastic, plastic adhesive strip, and/or medicinal (chlorophenolic).

☐ **Solvent** – Aromas and flavors of higher alcohols (fusel alcohols). Similar to acetone or lacquer thinner aromas.

☐ **Sour/Acidic** – Tartness in aroma and flavor. Can be sharp and clean (lactic acid), or vinegar-like (acetic acid).

☐ **Sulfur** – The aroma of rotten eggs or burning matches.

☐ **Vegetal** – Cooked, canned, or rotten vegetable aroma and flavor (cabbage, onion, celery, asparagus, etc.)

☐ **Yeasty** – A bready, sulfury or yeast-like aroma or flavor.

Appearance (as appropriate for style)   _____ / 3
Comment on color, clarity, and head (retention, color, and texture)

_____
_____
_____
_____

Flavor (as appropriate for style)   _____ /20
Comment on malt, hops, fermentation characteristics, balance, finish/aftertaste, and other flavor characteristics

_____
_____
_____
_____
_____
_____

Mouthfeel (as appropriate for style)   _____ / 5
Comment on body, carbonation, warmth, creaminess, astringency, and other palate sensations

_____
_____
_____
_____

Overall Impression   _____ /10
Comment on overall drinking pleasure associated with entry, give suggestions for improvement

_____
_____
_____
_____
_____
_____

Total   _____ /50

SCORING GUIDE		
Outstanding	(45 - 50):	World-class example of style.
Excellent	(38 - 44):	Exemplifies style well, requires minor fine-tuning.
Very Good	(30 - 37):	Generally within style parameters, some minor flaws.
Good	(21 - 29):	Misses the mark on style and/or minor flaws.
Fair	(14 - 20):	Off flavors/aromas or major style deficiencies. Unpleasant.
Problematic	(00 - 13):	Major off flavors and aromas dominate. Hard to drink.

	Stylistic Accuracy				
Classic Example	☐	☐	☐	☐	**Not to Style**
	Technical Merit				
Flawless	☐	☐	☐	☐	**Significant Flaws**
	Intangibles				
Wonderful	☐	☐	☐	☐	**Lifeless**

BJCP Beer Scoresheet   Copyright © 2012 Beer Judge Certification Program   rev. 120213   *Please send any comments to Comp_Director@BJCP.org*

Glossary

ABV (alcohol by volume): The amount of alcohol in a beer.

acetic acid: The acid in vinegar; occasionally found in sour beers, though usually considered a fault.

Acetobacter: The bacteria that produce acetic acid; activated when exposed to oxygen.

aldehyde: A chemical compound produced by the oxidation of alcohols.

autolysis: The process of yeast cell walls breaking down; releases a variety of flavors ranging from soy sauce to meaty to hazelnuts.

bottle-conditioning: The process of carbonating beer in the bottle through refermentation. Live yeast is retained in the beer.

Brettanomyces (brett): A naturally occurring wild yeast that can be used to ferment wort into beer. Traditionally used in the fermentation of lambic and other historical beer styles, more recently it has begun to be cultured and sold directly to brewers.

ester: A chemical compound resulting from the reaction of an alcohol and an acid. Most esters found in beer are fermentation by-products, but others are formed during aging processes. Typically described as "fruity."

foeder: A large oak vat used to ferment beer or wine. Typically used for the fermentation of Flanders red ales because the oak staves house the bacteria necessary to create the style's unique flavors.

fusel alcohol: An ethanol molecule that has additional carbon molecules. Responsible for the "alcoholic" or "boozy" aspects in a beer; also important for ester and aldehyde formation in aged beer.

higher alcohol: *See* fusel alcohol.

lactic acid: The acid in yogurt found in certain sour beer styles.

Lactobacillus: A bacteria that creates lactic acid from sugar; found in most sour beer styles.

lignin: Soluble portion of oak wood; responsible for the "oaky" flavors that are extracted from the alcohol.

Madeira: A fortified Portuguese wine that is intentionally oxidized and aged for years prior to sale. A common flavor descriptor for aged beer.

Maillard reaction: The browning effect responsible for the production of melanoidins. Observable as the process that gives toasted bread its characteristic browning and flavor.

melanoidins: Brown, flavorful pigment compounds found in beer. Can be produced from the kilning of malt or the kettle caramelization of wort when boiled. When oxidized, responsible for a beer's sweet sherry flavor.

oxidation: The loss of an electron from an oxygen-based molecule to another molecule. Common reaction in beer due to inherent oxygen and beer's relative lack of antioxidants. Responsible for many aging-derived flavors in beer ranging from papery to sherry to toffee to dried fruit.

Pediococcus: A bacteria that ferments lactic acid from sugar; found in most sour beer styles.

phenol: A chemical compound that is often a by-product of fermentation. Phenol flavors can range from clove and smoke to medicinal or plastic. When synthesized during a *Brettanomyces* fermentation, phenols can become "barnyardy."

reductones: Components in beer that reduce the potential for oxidation; most are commonly derived from melanoidins.

residual sugars: The amount of sugar (often malt derived) left in a beer after it has been fermented.

trans-2-nonenal: An aldehyde commonly found in aged beer; always considered a fault. Typically described as "stale" or "wet cardboard."

ullage: The increased headspace in a bottle of beer due to the evaporation of liquid through a dried-out cork.

vertical: A collection of different years of the same beer.

ACKNOWLEDGMENTS

I would like to thank all the wonderful people who make up the craft-brewing community. There is no other industry in the world whose members are so willing to share information for the greater good of us all. I'd particularly like to thank Chad Yakobson of Crooked Stave, Dr. Bill at Stone, Jean Van Roy at Cantillon, Vinnie Cirluzo of Russian River, Tomme Arthur of The Lost Abbey, Jim Crooks of Firestone Walker, Gabe Fletcher of Anchorage Brewing Company, Alan Sprints at Hair of the Dog, Steve Bruce at Toronado, Erik Peterson at Bull & Bush, Chris Black at Falling Rock Tap House, Peter Bouckaert at New Belgium, Billy Opinski at Humpy's Great Alaskan Alehouse, Maggie Campbell of Privateer, Scott Jennings and Bill Manley at Sierra Nevada, and Bill Young, the vintage beer specialist extraordinaire. I would also like to thank my tireless tasters: Lindsay Dawson, Aaron Muellenberg, Emily Parnell, Phillip Swearington, Courtney Rowes, Quintin Schermerhorn, and Kelli Schermerhorn. Last, I thank especially Storey Publishing, Margaret Sutherland in particular, for first believing in this book.

Index

BOLD = chart

A

ABV (alcohol by volume), 1, 10–11
acetic acid, 34, 53–54, 57, 73, 75, 140
Acetobacter, 53, 57, 75, 140
Adam old world ale, 23, 64
Akkurat Restaurant & Bar, 135–36
Alaskan Barley Wine Ale, 67
Alaskan Brewing Company, 11, 109
Alchemist, The, 32
alcohol, 36–37, 39, 40, 54. *See also*
    ABV and fusel alcohols
        low alcohol beers, 43
        oxidation, 46–48
Alcohol and Tobacco Tax and Trade
    Bureau (TTB), 124
aldehydes, 7, 36, 45–46, 48, 72, 139,
    140–41
AleSmith Old Numbskull, 64
amber-colored beers, 11, 88–89, 92,
    101
American beers and brewing, 37
American hops, 13, 30–31
American barley wines, 31, 60,
    70–71
        basic information, 64–67
        classic candidates, 67
        food pairings, 81
        Sierra Nevada Bigfoot, 88–90
        vs. English, 37, 63–64

Anchor Brewing Christmas Ale,
    103–5
Anchorage Brewing Company,
    55–56
Arctic Devil, 64
autolysis, 14, 50–51, 54, 67, 69, 95,
    140
Aventinus, 6, 36, 106–8
Avery Samael's Ale, 64

B

bacteria used in brewing, 32, 53, 57,
    73, 76, 140–41
Baltic porters, 60
barley malt, 18–19, 25
barley wine, 6, 21–22, 37. *See also*
    imperial stout
        American barley wines, 31, 60,
            63–67, 70–71, 81, 88–90
        English barley wines, 30, 37,
            60–64, 70–71, 81, 85–87
        food and vintage beer pairings,
            81
        hops in, 30–31
barrels and barrel-aging, 13, 41–44,
    53, 57
Beer Judge Certification Program
    (BJCP), 24, 29, 60
beer log, 121–22

143

Beer Scoresheet, 60, 139
Belgian golden ale, 21, **24**
Belgian quads, 21, 30, 44, 60, 83
    basic information, 70–73
    classic candidates, 72
    food pairings, 81
    Trappistes Rochefort 10,
      100–102
Belhaven, **24**, 29
Bell's beers, 6, 67–68, 70
Berliner Weisse, **24**, 57
Berserker Imperial Stout, 68, 70
Big Sky, 32
Bigfoot, 31, 45, 67, 88–90
Black Chocolate Stout, 70, 94–96
Blithering Idiot, 64
Boon Oude Geuze, 77, 79
bottle options
    closure, 15, 49
    corks, 15, 49, 114, 116–17
    green, clear, or brown, 15, 49
    orientation, 114, 118
    size, 15, 45
    wax, 114, 116–17
bottle-conditioned beer, 14, 21, 49,
    54, 88, 116, 118, 140, 144
Bourbon County Stout, 39, 70, 137
Brettanomyces (brett), 13–14, 31,
    53–56, 73, 76, 78–79, 109,
    140–41
Brick Store Pub, 133–34
Brooklyn Brewery Black Chocolate
    Stout, 70, 94–96
Brouwer's Cafe, 134–35
Bruery, The, 74–75
Bull & Bush Brewery, 129–30

C

Cafe Kulminator, 131–33
Campaign for Real Ale (CAMRA),
    51
Cantillon Classic Gueuze, **24**, 77,
    79, 132, 136
caramelization, 20–21, 63, 73, 141
carbonation, 49–50
cardboard flavor, 29, 31, 44, 46, 63,
    66, 69, 141
Cascade hops, **30**, 66, 88
cellar apps, 126–27
cellaring environment, 111–119. *See
    also* inventory
    bottle orientation, 118
    configurations, 116–17
    humidity, 114, 116
    insulated box, 118
    light exposure, 111, 113, 116–17
    refrigerated wine units, 116–17
    temperature, 111–113
Chimay Grande Réserve, 72,
    132–33, 136
chocolate stout, 22, 36, 67–68, 70,
    94–96
Coors Light, 1, **24**
corks, 15, 49
    prevent drying out, 114, 116–17
Courage Russian Imperial Stout,
    69–70
Crooked Stave, 55–56, 75

D

Dark Lord Imperial Stout, 70
De Cam Oude Geuze, 79
De Struise, 72, 132–33
decanting, 76

degradation
    hops, 28–29, 31, 46
    yeast, 67, 69
Delilah's, 136–37
Deschutes, 70, 75
Dogfish Head, 67
Doggie Claws, 67
doppelbock, 6, 9, **24**, 36, 106–107, 109
Double Barrel Ale, 41
Drie Fonteinen, 130, 135-36
    Oude Geuze, 79, 91–93
dubbel, 60, 70, 72, 100
Duvel, 2, 21, 24

E

East End, 84
Ebenezer's Restaurant & Pub, 131–32
Eldridge Pope, 64
English barley wines, 30, 37, 70–71
    basic information, 60–64
    classic candidates, 64
    food pairings, 81
    J.W. Lees Harvest Ale, 85–87
    vs. American, 37, 63–64
esters, 18, 21, 29, 140
    basic information, 31–36
    fruity quality, 13, 33–34, 47–48, 56, 63
European hops, 13
Excel, 122, 126
Expedition Stout, 68, 70

F

Falling Rock Taphouse, 130–31
fermentation temperature, 14–15, 32–33, 72

final gravity, **24**, 25
Firestone Walker Brewing Company, 41
Flanders ales, 14, 18, 34, 57, 60, 140
    basic information, 73–75
    food pairings, 81
    Rodenbach Grand Cru, 97–99
foeders, 73, 97, 140
food and vintage beer pairings, 81
Founders Imperial Stout, 70
Fresh Beer Only!, The, 124
freshness dating, 124
fruity yeast esters, 13, 33–36, 47–48, 56, 63
Fuggle hops, **30**, 94
Fuller Vintage Ale, 37, 64, 131, 134
fusel alcohols, 7, 11, 33, 36–37, 48

G

George Gale, 37
Girardin Gueuze, 79
Google Docs, 126
Goose Island, 39, 70, 137
Gouden Carolus, 72
Grand Cru
    Gouden Carolus, 72
    Rodenbach, 72, 97–99, 129
Gratitude, 84
gravity
    final gravity, **24**, 25
    high-gravity beer, 39, 48, 67
Great Divide, 42
gueuze, 14, **24**, 50, 54, 56, 60
    basic information, 76–80
    Cantillon Classic, **24**, 79, 132, 136
    classic candidates, 79

gueuze (*continued*)
    Drie Fonteinen Oude Geuze, 79, 91–93, 130, 135–36
    food pairings, 81
    perceived flavors of fresh vs. 10-year, **80**
Guinness, **24**

H

Hair of the Dog, 23, 64, 67, 135
Hallertau hops, 27, **30**, 107
Hanssens Oude Gueuze, 79
Heady Topper, 32
hefeweizens, 33, 35, 106
hops, 26–28, 30–31, 46
    American, 13, 30–31
    Cascade, **30**, 66, 88
    common hop varietals, **30**
    European, 13
    Fuggle, **30**, 94
    Hallertau, 27, **30**, 107
    Styrian Golding, **30**, 72
    Willamette, **30**, 94
Hopslam, 4, 6
hulupones, 28, 46
humidity of cellar, 114–117

I

imperial stout, 20–22, **24**, 31, 34, 42, 50–51, 60
    basic information, 67–70
    Brooklyn Brewery Black Chocolate Stout, 70, 94–96
    classic candidates, 70
    food pairings, 81
    ruined acidic, 50–51
insulated box, 118

inventory
    beer log, 121–22
    cellar apps, 126–27
    paper journal, 123–24
    spreadsheet, 126
IPA (India pale ale), 5–7, 13, 26–28, 30–32

J

J.W. Lees Harvest Ale, 64, 85–87, 130
Judgment Day, 73

K

Kabert, 133
kettle caramelization, 20–21, 63, 73, 141
kilned malt oxidation, 46

L

La Folie, 75
La Trappe, 70, 72
lactic acid, 10, 14, 53–54, 57, 73, 76, 140
Lactobacillus, 32, 53, 57, 73, 76, 140
lagers, 9, **24**, 36
    cellaring temperature, 14
    Schloss Eggenberg Samichlaus, 109
    yeasts, 31–33
Lagunitas Olde Gnarly Wine, 67
lambic style beer, 9, 14–15, 24, 51–57
    bottle orientation, 118
    cherry, 73, 79
    gueuzes, 76–79, 91–93
legs on a glass, 40

light exposure in cellars, 111, 113, 116–17
lignin, 42–43, 140
Lindemans Gueuze Cuvée René, 79
Lost Abbey, The, 53, 73, 75, 129

M

Madeira, 21, **61**, 63, 109, 141
magnum-style bottles, 2, 45, 103–5, 125
Maillard reaction, 20–21, 25, 141
malt, 19–28
    dark, 11, 14, 21, 50, 67, 70
    flavor changes, 11, 18
    kilned malt oxidation, 46
    Maris Otter, 25, 85
    melanoidins, 7, 20–21, 23, 25, 37
    roasted, 20–22, 37, 51, 67, 69, 81
    rules, 20–26
    smoked, 11, 36, 109
    Vienna and Munich, 19, 25
    vinegar, 18, 57, 75
Maris Otter malt, 25, 85
melanoidins, 7, 20–21, 23, 25, 37, 40, 46, 63, 141
microbiota, 18, 32, 49–51, 56–57, 73
Midnight Sun, 64, 70
Monk's Cafe, 136
Munich malt, 19, 25

N

New Belgium La Folie, 75
North Coast Old Stock Ale, 7, 64

O

oak barrel aging, 13, 41–44, 57, 73, 76
    beers aged in oak, 42, 92–93, 97–99
Odell Brewing Company, 44
Old Crustacean Barley Wine, 67
Old Numbskull, 64
Old Stock Ale, 7, 64
Olde Bluehair, 32
Olde Gnarly Wine, 67
Olde School Barleywine, 67
Ommegang, 73, 75
Origins, 75
Orval, 56, 109
Oude Gueuze
    Boon, 79
    Drie Fonteinen, 91–93
Oude Tart, 74–75
oxidation, 18, 22, 28–29, 43–48, 141

P

Panil Barriquée Sour, 75, 129
Pannepot, 72, 132
paper journal, 123–24
Pediococcus, 32, 53, 73, 76, 141
perceived flavors of fresh vs. 10-year gueuze, 80
phenols, 13–14, 18, 53–57
    basic information, 31–36
    oxidation effects, 44–45
Prize Old Ale, 37
proteins falling out, 12, 22, 63

Q

Quadrupel, 70, 72

R

rauchbiers, 13, 60
reactive oxygen species (ROS), 45–46
Red Poppy Ale, 74–75
reductones, 21, 63, 141
refrigerated wine units, 116–17
Reinheitsgebot law, 26
residual sugars, 22–25, 56, 63–64, 66–67, 69, 73, 75–76, 141
roasted flavors, 11, 20–22, 37, 51, 67, 69, 81
Rodenbach
    brewery, 73
    Grand Cru, 74–75, 97–99
Rogue Old Crustacean Barley Wine, 67
Rouge, Ommegang, 75
rules for aging beer, 10–15
Russian Imperial Stout, **24**, 69–70
Russian River, 28, 73

S

Saccharomyces cerevisiae, 49, 53–54, 56
Saison Dupont, 24
Salvation, 73
Schloss Eggenberg Samichlaus, 109
Schneider & Sohn Aventinus, 6, 36
    basic information, 106–8
Scoresheet, Beer, 60, 139
Scottish ale, 20, 24, 29
Sierra Nevada, **24**
    Bigfoot, 31, 67, 88–90
smoked beer, 10–11, 36, 109
Smoked Porter, 11, 109

Smuttynose Barleywine Style Ale, 58, 67
Soleil de Minuit, 135
sour beer, 10, 14, 51–54, 57
    bottle orientation, 118
    Drie Fonteinen Oude Geuze, 91–93
    Flanders red and brown ales, 73–78
    Rodenbach Grand Cru, 97–98
spreadsheet for inventory, 126
Stone Imperial Russian Stout, **24**, 70
stout, 11, 22, **24**, 31, 34, 36
    Brooklyn Brewery Black Chocolate Stout, 94–96
    chocolate, 22, 36, 67–68, 70, 94–96
    Goose Island Bourbon County Stout, 39, 70, 137
    Great Divide Yeti, 42
    imperial stout, 67–70
Styrian Golding hops, **30**, 72

T

tasting, 7, 59, 126
    Beer Scoresheet, 60, 139
    vertical, 7, 83–84, 108, 141
    Vintage Beer Tasting Wheel, **61**
temperature
    cellar, 84, 111–13, 116–17
    fermentation, 14–15, 32–33, 72
    kilning malt, 19, 22, 25, 46
    pasteurization, 49
    remote thermostat, 113
    slow roasting, 39

swings, protection against, 45, 119

The Fresh Beer Only!, 124

thermostat, remote, 113

Third Coast Old Ale, 67

Thomas Hardy's Ale, 4, 6, 37–38, 64, 124, 130–31

Three Floyds, 70

Three Philosophers, 73

Toronado, 128–29

trans-2-nonenal, 29, 30–31, 44, 46, 141

Trappistes Rochefort 10, 7, 23, 71, 73

    basic information, 100–102

tripel, 21, 60, 70

U

ullage, 114–115, 141

umami flavor, 50, 86

unpasteurized beers, 14, 49, 51

V

vertical

    tasting, 7, 83–84, 108, 141

    vs. horizontal bottle orientation, 118

Vienna malt, 19, 25

vinegar sourness from acetic acid, 53, 57, 75, 97, 140

vintage beer

    rules, 10–15

    tasting wheel, **61**

vintage kegs, 45, 129–30, 134

vintage-beer bars, 128–37

    Akkurat Restaurant & Var, 135–36

    Brick Store Pub, 133–34

Brouwer's Cafe, 134–35

Bull & Bush Brewery, 129–30

Cafe Kulminator, 131–33

Delilah's, 136–37

Ebenezer's Restaurant & Pub, 131–32

Falling Rock Taphouse, 130–31

Monk's Cafe, 136

other notable bars, 137

Toronado, 128–29

virgin barrels, 44

W

wax, bottle, 114, 116–17

Weizenbock, 106

    Schneider & Sohn Aventinus, 106–8

Westvleteren, 73, 83, 133

wet-cardboard flavor, 29, 31, 44, 46, 63, 66, 69, 141

Weyerbacher, 64

wheat beer, 12–13, 19, 36, 57

Willamette hops, **30**, 94

wood aging, 13, 18, 41–44, 52, 73

Woodcut No. 5, 44

Y

yeast, 49, 50–51, 53

    Brettanomyces wild yeast, 13–14, 31, 53–56, 73, 76, 78–79, 109, 140–41

    esters and phenols, 13, 18, 31–36, 47–48

    fruity esters, 13, 33–36, 47–48, 56

    Saccharomyces cerevisiae, 49, 53–54, 56

Yeti, 42

Explore the Flavors of Beer

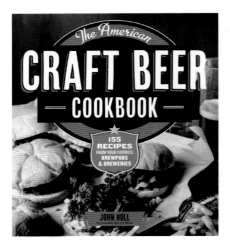

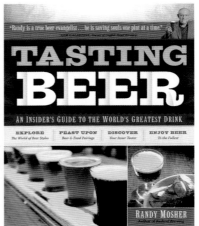

The American Craft Beer Cookbook
by John Holl

The best beer-friendly recipes from breweries, brewpubs, and taverns across the United States.

352 pages. Paper. ISBN 978-1-61212-090-4.

Tasting Beer by Randy Mosher

The first comprehensive guide to tasting, appreciating, and understanding the world's best drink — craft beers.

256 pages. Paper. ISBN 978-1-60342-089-1.